REFLECTIONS ON THE GLOBAL VILLAGE

Opinion and Analysis

REFLECTIONS ON THE GLOBAL VILLAGE

Opinion and Analysis

DAVID MONYAE

REAL AFRICAN PUBLISHERS

REAL AFRICAN PUBLISHERS

Published by Real African Publishers
PO Box 3317
Houghton
Johannesburg 2041

www.realafricanpublishers.com

First published in June 2021

© David Monyae

ISBN 978-1-928341-95-6

Editor: Angela McClelland
Production editor: Reedwaan Vally
Cover design: Adam Rumball

In memory of my mother,
Wilhelmina Motatjo Maake,
1935–2020

For Lindiwe, Lennon and Thandwa

Contents

Interlude   109

African Politics   113

South African Politics   **185**

Personal Political   **199**

Acknowledgements

This book would not have been possible without the help of members of my family and friends, at home and abroad, whose assistance – large and small – allowed me to think and discuss ideas in the last few years.

I owe an enormous debt of gratitude to those who gave me detailed and constructive comments in one way or another, including Mbongeni Myende, Bhaso Ndzendze, Emmanuel Matambo, Sizo Nkala, Lebo Mosebua, Zizipho Masiza, Charles Matseke, Bongane Gasela and Gibson Banda. I'm also immensely grateful to the Centre for Africa-China Studies at the University of Johannesburg for allowing me to focus on Africa and the role of external actors – as well as for their support and generous funding of this project.

I want to acknowledge Angela McClelland and Reedwaan Vally of Real African Publishers, who constantly encouraged me to 'get this book done'.

Above all, I would like to thank my wife Lindiwe for her love and constant support. Thank you for being my editor, proofreader and sounding board. I owe you everything.

List of Abbreviations

4IR	Fourth Industrial Revolution
AfCFTA	African Continental Free Trade Area
Africa CDC	Africa Centre for Disease Control
Agoa	African Growth and Opportunity Act
AI	Artificial Intelligence
AIIB	Asian Infrastructure Investment Bank
AU	African Union
BRI	Belt and Road Initiative
Brics	Brazil, Russia, India, China, South Africa
CCP	Chinese Communist Party
Ciftis	China International Fair for Trade in Services
DRC	Democratic Republic of the Congo
EAC	East African Community
Ecowas	Economic Community of West African States
EU	European Union
Focac	Forum on China-Africa Cooperation
HCSEC	Huawei Cyber Security Evaluation Centre
IDFC	International Development Finance Corporation
IEBC	Independent Electoral and Boundaries Commission
IEC	Independent Electoral Commission
IISS	International Institute for Strategic Studies
IMF	International Monetary Fund
JSCI	Joint Standing Committee on Intelligence
LPA	Lagos Plan of Action
MDC	Movement for Democratic Change
NAM	Non-aligned Movement
NDB	New Development Bank
Nepad	New Partnership for Africa's Development
OECD	Organisation for Economic Co-operation and Development
Pida	Programme for Infrastructure Development in Africa
PRC	People's Republic of China
Quad	Quadrilateral Security Dialogue
RECs	Regional Economic Communities
SADC	Southern African Development Community
SAPs	Structural Adjustment Programmes
SSA	State Security Agency
Ticad	Tokyo International Conference on African Development
UJ	University of Johannesburg
UNHCR	UN High Commission for Refugees
WHO	World Health Organisation

Foreword

It has been my great pleasure to know David Monyae for 25 years: first as a friend and student, then as an author. He is a unique African voice who offers insight into the complex and challenging terrain of African international relations. He is a committed anticolonialist and internationalist who is acutely aware of the history of the great powers' exploitation of Africa and how that helped rob its peoples of their rightful heritage and prosperity. Likewise, he is steeped in the ways that states and inter-state organisations and their leaders have struggled for their self-interest and, occasionally, that of the public throughout the continent.

David's training has been to understand the ways that realpolitik shapes our world. By temperament, he recognises the common humanity of our frail and fallible species, and his aspiration is to improve the lot of the voiceless in world affairs by seeking to improve the quality of the policies and strategies of the continent's (and the world's) most powerful.

David's portrayal of the continent reveals several interrelated themes: Africa is beset by problems as diverse as climate change, corruption, wars and poverty. Yet, it retains enormous potential, which can be realised by multilateral cooperation and trade. What follows is a recent history of a continent's problems and promise, a chronicle of how states and international actors are both a cause for hope and suffering.

In his view, China has a positive role to play in African affairs. It can offset the traditional economic and military power of the West, who often act as if the era of colonialism is not yet past. Chinese investment and technology can help develop the continent, and Africans have much to learn from Chinese development.

For the Sino-African potential to be realised, the Chinese people will need to study the history of how Africans and outsiders have stumbled and succeeded. I can think of no better place to begin that study than with Comrade David Monyae.

— John Hinshaw, Professor of History, Politics and Global Affairs at Lebanon Valley College in Annville, Pennsylvania

Introduction

Black people, African people, people from the Global South and those who don't come from the traditional West have always been viewed as infantile. They were not to be trusted or allowed to self-ascribe or self-govern. That was the premise responsible for colonialism, imperialism and apartheid and the rhetoric and spin they left behind as a persisting legacy to this day.

Our stories, journeys, histories, politics and dialogues are, as a result, never our own but echo the distorted refrain of those who sought to name and claim us not as people but as property ... for our property. To declare that our oral traditions are archaic, unsophisticated and savage. Then theirs methodically appear as factual, empirical and handsome, when that is the furthest thing from the truth. They proposed that our legacies, spoken through poetry, song and our very names carried inadequacies and could not be reliable as a source of legitimate historical archive – the truth that was cascaded down from God to each and every individual as not only a beautiful story of individual, communal and societal history but also as a birthright. Each and every life was accounted for in the verses and stanzas that made up the language, traditions and culture of African peoples.

You see, in misrepresenting someone's language, culture and identity, the endgame is to control their history. The reason that is important is that when an individual or group controls the history of another, the other loses their agency. Their sovereignty is eroded and, before long, the misinformation leads to widespread behaviour control: the individual's view of the world and themselves (whether it is true or not) is in someone else's hands – and they can use it to their benefit and do. That was the rationale for using the Bible as a tool for oppression.

Governance seems always to have a mutually complicit relationship with the press or media centred on oppression and subjugating people to others' will. A hegemony on people's narrative has always been the objective. Systematic and deliberate actions have been taken through centuries to steer attitudes about one group by another through governments and the press. Consider the settlers arriving in the Cape brandishing the gospel as a weapon for dominance and their British and European Press counterparts' weekly accounts from the 'New World'. Consider, still, Verwoerd's Nazi-inspired apartheid and the brainwashing of generations of Black, brown and white people through heavily skewed education policies. Finally, consider the Black ruling majority and their vacuum in terms of a consistent narrative about who and what we are and how we should view the world.

When they made landfall and created their colonies, the objective for Europeans was to diminish those they encountered to subhuman status. That was the only way to 'discover' a land that was already occupied. They figured that if they could convince themselves and those they found there that they were not human, then they were technically the first people to settle there, and therefore the land was indeed not stolen but discovered. That proved easy when converting people to Christianity and then showing them a white Jesus. If man is made in God's image and he looks white, then Black people cannot qualify to be men (human). On the contrary, white people are made in Jesus's image because he appears white on all illustrations, and they are therefore close to him, but Black people are not and are the furthest thing from Jesus. Hence the nickname that was given to Black people from the Arabic term that means non-believer: ungodly, subhuman and childlike.

Jan Smuts, while addressing the Civic Forum Town Hall in New York City on 9 January 1930, proclaimed to the audience of 1,500 that Africans were docile animals, the most patient of animals, next to the ass. He went on to describe 'natives' as 'happy-go-lucky', 'childlike with a child psychology', 'good-tempered' and 'carefree' people who loved 'wine and song' and who had no original religious beliefs, literature or art or desire to improve themselves. That is the view that the settlers and their European and American counterparts had and needed to have of Africans and needed the Africans to have as well. It is the only way they could rule us virtually uncontested for so long: they controlled the narrative.

In 1948, Verwoerd was successful in ushering in his policy of apartheid. But more importantly, he was borrowing a page from his hero, Joseph Goebbels (Nazi Germany's Minister of Public Enlightenment and Propaganda), who was able to galvanise stereotypes and mild prejudices and, through propaganda, convince a continent that their murderous reign was justified. Using the same logic and flavour of violence and carefully curated white supremacist ideology as his Third Reich role model, he implemented a school system that was to create generations of subservient, uneducated and compliant Black people through a severely underfunded Bantu Education – along with generations of entitled, privileged and out of touch white people – through the majority of the state's budget being spent on less than 20 per cent of the population. We are still in the clutches of the mental shackles that he put in place. More so because, outside of the isolated Steve Biko and Robert Sobukwe, no one has ever attempted to remove them.

After 1994, two campaigns existed: one with a tag line 'Peace in our land' and the other a 'Rainbow Nation'. Peace in our land, with its accompanying song and logo of two doves carrying an olive branch, was a direct response to the brewing civil war between the ANC and the IFP. The Rainbow Nation was Archbishop Desmond Tutu's brainchild as an opposing method for the racial hatred that was still evident after migration to a new democratic dispensation. He saw the effects of that hatred first-hand as Chair of the Truth and Reconciliation Commission and in his ministries in and around South African townships during some of the most tumultuous times in our history. A drive to embrace the diversity that had for so long broken South Africa was needed to heal it. Both campaigns worked. The fuse of war in Gauteng and KZN was extinguished, and Black and white people were tolerant of each other around the Rainbow Nation banner. But not for long. After years of an absent message or rhetoric for South Africans to rally behind, divisions sown by racist legacies reared their ugly heads again. The Black ruling majority didn't have anything for people to rally behind in nation-building or even shaping an ideology, as did their regime predecessors.

That is when our stories shifted from being authored by us to foreign publications and viewpoints being the foremost authorities about us. The dominant voices that told of us were not ours. Scholars, academics – even media houses publishing the leading newspapers in the country and across the continent – showed an obvious bias towards the dominant narrative of African disparity. Development and prosperity were not as popular as the poor starving children with flies on their face.

There exists a contestation of ideas and rhetoric about politics and African politics, in particular. That means that the multitude of interests from the international community on African issues is directed towards showing a people who cannot and must not govern themselves. Their resources and material potential or even position in the world must be held by other nations to be productive and efficient. That is the aim of the dominant voices that tell Africa's story and bring Africa the world's story.

We, the people, need a voice – a voice that is vital to fulfilling two distinct objectives: it must enable us to tell our stories, and it must be able to carry our stories to the world and deliver them the way we intended – to export our essence far and wide with our traditions, experiences and thoughts intact. Second, and equally important, that voice must bring us news of the world in a way that appeals to our collective understanding and susceptibilities – which means that we need one of ours to tell us about the world without any preconceived ulterior motives. They must be able to relay knowledge of the world for dynamic dialogue from an African departure point – understanding how a certain tone and style, projected in a certain manner, might evoke a favourable or unfavourable reaction.

We know now that we cannot merely trust the altruism of other people's translations of other lands and their people. Like them, we need to start listening to our voices and elevate them to where they have dominion over our lived experiences and not someone else's. We need one or more of us to set the scene and paint with the vivid colours of West African sepia, umber and terracotta. They need to fashion our tales with shades and textures of raw emotion; make them hear ululating joy and wailing sorrow. They must speak with a sun-scorched tongue, words flashing and loud as if born of a rolling Highveld thunderstorm. They must be a window turned gateway for others to almost feel the rich black piece of earth on which our home sits and helps us to see and feel theirs.

This anthology offers us that voice. The following is a guide through global politics from the unique vantage point of the individuals and communities that those politics affect. It is an attempt to offer a view that has African interests and only African interests at heart. It is a narration of subject matter from the inner depths of our own to far-flung lands, which nonetheless have a profound effect on us. This edition of the common text about us and the rest of the world offers a balance – one that can counter the so-called facts and analyses from specialists and experts about people they know very little about. It peers beyond the everyday humdrum of poor Africa but offers the fears and joys, resolute in the face of uncertainty that accompanies the policies and amendments that are authored by the well-suited and heeled officials and bureaucrats. That is the view that takes into account the conversation that it will spark in the queue in a taxi rank or the barber shop-come-tent with a headshot of Tupac Shakur on the front.

There was a need to offer discussion and dialogue on global politics to audiences outside of the usual academic and scholarly ecosystems harboured in university corridors. The institutions of higher learning gained notoriety for forcing knowledge creation from their students, only to have that knowledge collect dust in monumental libraries when they graduate – unless to occasionally use their knowledge to reinforce their self-importance to alienate the very people they studied and studied for. It defeated the objective of learning to be able to tell our stories; of being the pride of a community because finally, one wore a hood and was educated. What was it for if not to serve the people in that community? This book gives the people who are the less-celebrated players in global politics a chance to tell and listen to their stories. By reading about migration, refugees, xenophobia and bilateral and multilateral economic agreements, they get to be part of the conversation and dialogue.

This book is split into four focus areas, namely: Global Politics, African Politics, South African Politics, and the Personal Political.

- Global Politics covers subjects that deal with global shifts like the US presidential election; the economic cold war between China and the US; Boris Johnson and whether he will deliver on Brexit and how. It is meant to inform about global powers and their relationships as they relate to us and the possible unintended consequences of their relationships for us.
- African Politics covers subjects such as 'Where to from here for Zimbabwe?'; 'China-Africa trade expo a unique opportunity for Africa'; 'AU must take ownership of African matters'. Those are subjects specific to the upliftment of Africa, either by informing of possible pitfalls that other countries are headed towards because of the experience of another, or highlighting possible development deals with first-world powers that could benefit Africa.
- South African Politics is about our foreign policy, including 'SA's golden opportunity to uplift Africa'; 'IEC a laudable example to Africa's democracies'; 'SA, Nigeria must tackle xenophobia'. Those pieces are predominantly about South Africa and its relationships with its neighbours. It tells of how we can contribute to our neighbourhood positively and of us being stronger as a result of having more robust regional counterparts.
- The Personal Political is about politics that don't belong to any state or international institution but still qualify as global politics. It includes 'Is Pik Botha deserving of a state funeral?'; 'Gluttony and crass materialism killed Ubuntu'; 'We've done well but we can do better'. This section is about the personal experience of people and their image in the global arena and whether those two images can be reconciled. In the case of Pik Botha and South Africa, the feelings have proven challenging to coexist. Globally, both are marvelled and lauded for various positive contributions, but peoples lived experiences tell a vastly different story.

Geopolitics

Epidemic exposes West's colonial mentality

Xenophobia, ideological bias and the West's fear of China's rise are the triple burdens that hinder the fight against the Novel Coronavirus outbreak in China. Recently, Kevin Rudd, former Australian prime minister and president of the Asia Society Policy Institute in New York, wrote: 'The wider world should show sympathy and express solidarity with the long-suffering Chinese people. These are ugly times, and the racism implicit (and sometimes explicit) in many responses to Chinese people around the world makes me question just how far we have really come as a human family.'

Indeed, Rudd's take on the need for a people-centred global approach in the fight against the epidemic resonates with a well-known African idiom commonly used among the Nguni dialects, which says *Inxeba lendoda alihlekwa*: 'The wound of a man is not laughed at.'

In reporting on the Novel Coronavirus, *The Wall Street Journal* carried an article by Bard College Professor Walter Russell Mead titled 'China is the Real Sick Man of Asia'. The learned professor and the newspaper in question are quite aware that the term 'sick man of Asia' is a derogatory phrase that emanates from China's century of humiliation at the hands of Western and Japanese powers: it was commonly used by the foreign forces who conquered China to justify their inhumane treatment of Chinese people.

That colonial language was also common in Africa when colonial masters considered their religion, culture and general lifestyle to be superior to those of the indigenous people whom they perceived to be disease-ridden and unclean.

There have also been attacks against the attempts of the Chinese authorities to speedily control the outbreak that were cloaked in ideological clothes. There have been numerous opinion pieces across the Western media that have used the breakout of this disease to directly attack the Chinese system.

The main aim of such attacks is to advance the long-held view that liberal democracies handle and manage epidemics and general crises much better than what is considered to be an authoritarian regime in China. The weakness of such an argument lies in the fact that it is ahistorical. The United States itself is littered with endless mismanagement of epidemics and general crises confronted by its people. A recent example is Hurricane Katrina in New Orleans in 2005. The George W. Bush administration failed dismally to respond to the crisis that affected almost 80 per cent of the city's mainly Black population.

The British *Guardian* newspaper carried an article by Emma Graham-Harrison on 31 January in which she said that 'China soon won international plaudits for a huge mobilisation, including the near-impossible feat of building two new hospitals in as many weeks, even as Wuhan became an international byword for a new epidemic'. She further settled for ideological point-scoring: 'Yet, as information about the early days of the outbreak has slowly filtered out of China, it has become increasingly clear that the same political system that allowed Beijing to order such a dramatic response also initially allowed the virus to foster.'

Additionally, some elements in the Western media and US officials are using the epidemic as a tool in their bid to limit the rise of China. On 24 January, *Foreign Policy* magazine unashamedly carried an article titled 'Welcome to the Belt and Road Pandemic'. And US Secretary of Commerce Wilbur Ross, responding to the epidemic in China, was quoted as saying 'I think it will help to accelerate the return of jobs to America'.

At this critical juncture in the fight against the Novel Coronavirus, there is a need to build a united front in combating the spread of the disease as well as finding a cure. The African continent, in particular, has worked tirelessly with China within the Forum on China-Africa Cooperation on managing communicative diseases. Africa can assist China in its efforts to manage the virus. Africa has responded soberly to the outbreak of the Novel Coronavirus in China without causing unnecessary panic. But more efforts ought to be taken to strengthen African health workers' ability to respond to the virus, should it spread across the continent. Africa should also reject the triple Western diseases of xenophobia, ideological bias and fear of China's rise.

There's no evidence that China and Huawei pose any threat to Africa

Investigative journalist Heidi Swart poses the question of whether South Africans are safe with Huawei. From her previous articles, one can rightfully conclude that she has her mind made up: Huawei is a threat to security and privacy. Swart's latest article, 'Are South Africans safe with Huawei? It's all about the risk' (*Daily Maverick*, 5 March 2020), the first part of two, is an impressive illustration of how Huawei has grown from its founding in 1987. Indubitably, one of the significant factors behind Huawei's astounding growth is its proximity to the Chinese government. That close relationship has seen Huawei score massive, lucrative deals from the Chinese government. Huawei's founder, Ren Zhengfei, worked in the People's Liberation Army, and that experience partly explains why his franchise has close ties to the government of China.

While Huawei's proximity to the Chinese government has been instrumental in the company's breathtaking expansion, it has left China's national and technological competitors unnerved. Swart's article apportioned most of its attention toward America's response and misgivings about Huawei's growing footprint in the technological sphere. Perhaps reasonably, the US government is convinced that Huawei will be used by China to conduct espionage, harvest data illegally, hack into foreign trade secrets and steal intellectual property.

A plethora of American voices have looked askance at China's technology inroads. Even the arrest of Huawei CFO and Ren's daughter, Meng Wanzhou, was arguably demonstrative of Western efforts to curtail Huawei's and China's development. The avalanche of protests from the Chinese government over the arrest provided fodder for people who look at Huawei as a hidden arm of the Chinese government's surveillance tentacles.

Swart did an admirable job in providing a litany of measures that the US has taken to occlude Huawei's alleged intrusion on privacy. She did equally well in providing information that links Huawei and its personnel to the Chinese government but very little evidence about the safety and risk threats in South Africa. I hope that Part Two of her article will answer the question that is relevant to an African and South African audience amid the mudslinging between Huawei and its Western detractors: whither Africa?

Without attempting to pre-empt Swart's response, which is foregone, judging from her previous articles, Africa should exercise vigilance in its consumption of foreign products, Western or otherwise. Swart's Part One does not delve into implications for South Africans who use Huawei products. I would guess that the first piece was providing the context for the second piece, which will pointedly outline how Huawei is a real safety and risk threat to South Africa. If indeed Huawei is a rogue enterprise doing the Chinese government's bidding, the consequences could be dire in South Africa, where Huawei claims almost 29 per cent of the total mobile market.

The most crucial player in the consumption of technology in South Africa should be the country itself. Articles such as the one written by Swart should be scrutinised and lent context where lacking. For example, no one would expect the US government to speak glowingly about its most formidable competitor, regardless of Huawei's blemishes, which do exist. Meng's arrest, for example, came at the time when the US and China were locked in the throes of the trade war.

Furthermore, due to its officious stance towards the developing world, the West has forfeited its allure in Africa, an erosion compounded by Donald Trump's cantankerous presidency. What that does is enhance China's image in Africa's eyes, the result of which is the gain being made by Chinese behemoths such as Huawei. South Africa knows that it has to be vigilant in consuming tech products from outside. Still, for that, it does not need foreign tutelage, and it does not require the encouragement of opinions, albeit from South Africa, that are suspiciously biased. In any case, Western surveillance the world over is well documented, so shunning Huawei and opting for Western products does not insulate one from oversight.

What makes China and its enterprises more attractive to South Africa, as Swart correctly notes, is that South Africa and China share cordial relations, unlike with the US. That said, Huawei is as much a security issue as it is a political and diplomatic one. Trump's presidency and rhetoric, laced with insular bombast, and the UK's withdrawal from the European Union, demonstrate Western retreat from the charge of globalisation. China has proved to be trending in the opposite direction, in tandem with Africa.

Thus, US concerns over Huawei and China should never be automatically assumed to be Africa's concerns. It is understandable that the US, a country that for three-quarters of a century stood virtually unchallenged at the summit of the global pecking order, should be reluctant to be challenged by an ambitious China, a country that a few generations ago was a Third World backwater. Also, as Hilary Clinton notes in her 2017 book *What Happened,* technology will dominate many spheres of life in the twenty-first century, including warfare. Naturally, the US wants to be a principal architect of the emerging order, and it takes umbrage at the fact that Africans seem to opt for China and its technology products to the detriment of the US and its goods.

Allegations that the Chinese government is using Huawei to collect and steal information are not likely to find a sympathetic ear in Africa, especially if such allegations come from an increasingly paranoid US presided over by a man whose dislike of China is barely concealed. In terms of China's support for Huawei, that is expected in much the same way as one would expect the United States government to support their private companies.

In South Africa's case, the country is sovereign and has the right to choose what products to consume and from whom without pandering to blackmail or slander from competitors who want to penetrate the continent. Is a perceived or manufactured threat of safety and risk to the US also a de facto threat to South Africa? While the article makes a loaded US government case against Huawei as a threat to that country, it hardly shows the evidential risk to South Africa, so far. For now, we will wait for Heidi Swart's Part Two.

Work in concert to contain virus

On 15 March, President Cyril Ramaphosa delivered a speech to the nation about the Coronavirus. South Africa has 62 confirmed cases of the virus, with the number expected to increase.

The speech was a commendable effort by a visibly sombre head of state. In terms of the Disaster Management Act, he declared the Coronavirus a national disaster and went on to list a raft of stringent measures designed to mitigate its spread. Those measures included immediate visa cancellations for countries that have been identified as high risk and foreign nationals who have visited high-risk areas in the last 20 days. Within South Africa, the government has discouraged large gatherings, which increase the spread of the virus.

The president's speech merits admiration because it was based on sound science. However, apart from national measures, the Coronavirus teaches something about the nature of the international political economy. In the US, Donald Trump could not resist the temptation to inject racial and nationalistic undertones into the current crisis.

Quite inexplicably, he described Covid-19 as 'The Chinese virus', a remark that, needless to say, drew a lot of criticism from people who perceived his gratuitous description as racist. Another interesting thing to emerge from the current crisis is that there seems to be more social and personal interaction between the West and China, unlike what has been assumed about Africa and China. Indeed, the cases that emerged in South Africa were contracted through people who had visited mainly Western countries such as Italy, Austria, France and Canada, rather than China.

Italy raises a number of questions about cohesion in the West and the place of globalisation. That country seems to have been abandoned by its Nato and EU allies, partly because the US and UK are under nationalistic leaderships who are averse to globalisation.

It is telling that countries of the Global South, such as Cuba and China, have demonstrated more eagerness to help an embattled Italy. It is hoped that after the spread has been controlled and Italy recovers, the leaders of that country will appreciate the fact that the world is largely integrated.

Circumstances such as the emergence Covid-19 remind us that we should work in concert to contain challenges that threaten the world. Covid-19 should galvanise efforts for medical research, which will be crucial, especially in Africa where health systems battle to contain more common diseases. While globalisation is becoming less popular in the Western world, the Global South seems to be bucking that trend, and Africa is a good example.

The African Continental Free Trade Area, the largest of its kind in the world, demonstrates that the African continent seeks to be more integrated. That, however, will entail helping poorer African countries to meet the basic needs of their citizens.

When Ramaphosa delivered his national disaster address, his manner was dignified, depicting much-needed statesmanship under trying circumstances.

It should also not be forgotten that South Africa Chairs the AU in 2020. When coupled with its comparatively sophisticated technology and health care system in Africa, it is only natural that other African countries will look to South Africa for advice and direction.

For the government to succeed in that daunting endeavour and inspire the rest of the continent, it will need the collaboration and compliance of all stakeholders – from the private sector, education institutions and civil society to ordinary citizens. When all of those actors are pulling in the same direction, South Africa can succeed in its efforts.

Covid-19: Ramaphosa has shown he has what it takes

The unprecedented global crisis caused by Covid-19 unfolding in Italy, the US, UK, China, South Korea and on our shores has the potential to change our lives and international relations fundamentally.

The most notable feature of leadership during a crisis is the ability to unite a family, community or nation around a straightforward programme of action. In any society, people measure the quality of leadership in times such as the one at hand by the clarity of messages, command, policy direction and, more importantly, unity of purpose. What distinguishes Covid-19 from other crises is that it threatens the very survival of nations and therefore demands that leaders at national and international levels work in unison to provide clear direction to their countries and the world.

When the world was faced with the threat of fascism during World War 2, it responded by building a robust global coalition of freedom fighters to defeat the enemy. Now, once again, we are faced by a grave threat to world peace and security. This time, it is not a traditional visible enemy such as Adolf Hitler but a biological pandemic.

Judging by the unfolding events, particularly in developed countries, especially the US, it appears that global leadership remains absent. The Covid-19 pandemic couldn't have come at a worse time: most institutions of global political and economic governance such as the UN, International Monetary Fund (IMF) and World Bank are on the brink of collapse.

The US and China, the world's two largest economies, are currently bickering over ideological issues, trade, technologies, the South China Sea and, most recently, the origin of Covid-19 itself.

The EU has dismally failed to provide much-needed leadership as Italy grapples with high Covid-19 fatalities. Where else can the world expect sound leadership? What about emerging markets, especially Brazil, Russia, India, China and South Africa (Brics) under the chairmanship of President Jair Bolsonaro?

Equally, Brics exists only in name and on paper: the group haven't risen to fill the global leadership vacuum. Like other formations such as the G7 and EU, Brics appear clueless on how to respond to the current global health crisis. As it stands, Brics countries other than China are mostly limiting their responses.

The sheer lack of leadership at the global level sadly signals the final nail in the coffin of the post-1945 world order. During World War 2, the West and East (with different ideological outlooks) set their differences aside to confront the menace. US President Harry S. Truman, British Prime Minister Winston Churchill, Soviet leader Joseph Stalin and South Africa's General Jan Smuts had a joint plan to roll back Axis powers.

President Donald Trump's White House press briefings are increasingly turning into comedy shows.

President Cyril Ramaphosa has indeed won the hearts and minds of his people and beyond. Although he gave a chilling speech, he demonstrated the leadership that is lacking at the global level. South Africa is not the US, UK or China; it does not command the resources of those countries. But Ramaphosa has risen to the occasion.

Like he did when negotiating the democratic transition in the 1990s, Ramaphosa has again brought all role-players together to contribute meaningfully to combating this unprecedented threat to the nation. As the AU chairperson, Ramaphosa ought to find ways of reaching out to the rest of Africa in the fight against Covid-19. With its poor health infrastructure, Africa remains the most vulnerable, so in the absence of global unity in combating Covid-19, drastic measures such as those taken by Ramaphosa are needed at the continental level.

A serious crisis will never go to waste

'You never let a serious crisis to go to waste. And what I mean by that, it's an opportunity to do things you think you could not do before.'

Those words were uttered by (former US) President Barack Obama's former chief of staff, Rahm Emanuel, at the height of the 2008 global financial crisis. Similarly, South Africa and the rest of the world face yet another monumental crisis prompted by Covid-19.

A new world order will certainly rise out of the ashes of this crisis with unique sets of challenges for individuals, business, civil society and states. That will require policymakers to simultaneously take appropriate measures to prepare people and the state for those changes, which will be felt in the ways people relate. The physical distancing encouraged to combat Covid-19 will usher in an unprecedented use of digital tools for interactions. The use of hard cash will give way to electronic banking. Similarly, e-commerce and e-learning will be prioritised over our traditional business and educational culture of physical interactions.

Covid-19 will also have a direct negative impact on democracy in that individuals will more likely be willing to surrender some aspects of their sovereignty and freedom for the betterment of society.

States and corporations will gain more power over individuals. That new normal means that an individual's personal information – such as health status, who one meets and where one has travelled – become critical determinants for security clearance.

The Covid-19 outbreak will provide states with a golden opportunity to accumulate more power as they introduce and enforce new security measures that will, to an extent, undermine some of the fundamental elements of the current freedoms as defined by liberal democracy.

It is therefore imperative for people to think deeply and innovatively about how to navigate those profound changes to their security and their implications on the Constitution. Civil society will be required to think hard and to avoid falling into a reactive mode. Change is unavoidable; therefore ideas of how to actively participate in shaping the new order will be more important than demonstrations in the streets.

There are clear market signals that the way the world does business will change. Some sectors will be more adversely affected than others. Business is already shedding jobs. South Africa is not immune to those global trends, and our businesses will have to adjust to those changes to survive. That means that our traditional sense of security will go beyond the current obsession of amassing armies and weapons against invading foreign enemies. The sophisticated weapons carrying nuclear warheads have already been made irrelevant in the face of the invisible Coronavirus.

The world's undisputed superpower, the US, has been caught napping and embarrassingly unable to protect its citizens from Covid-19. For instance, the top nuclear-powered US aircraft carrier *USS Theodore Roosevelt* was recently halted because some of its 5,000 troops were infected with Covid. That indeed poses the question about what constitutes security and reminds us all that, while it is essential to defend ourselves from external enemies, protecting one's population from invisible forces such as Covid-19 and climate change is equally important.

For South Africa's policymakers, specifically, the crisis should not be put to waste. It provides state, business, civil society and individuals with an opportunity to do things, as Rahm Emanuel stated, 'you think you could not do before'.

And that means learning lessons beyond the developed countries for survival. It is vital to find new ideas within African culture.

Pretoria News: Opinion / 15 April 2020

Racism must not strain SA's Sino ties

The recent distressing acts of racism meted out against Black Africans in Guangzhou, China, prompted a close friend to send a loaded text message to me: 'We want to see a strong statement from southern Africa's leading expert on Sino affairs.' First and foremost, racism and xenophobia must be condemned in the strongest terms, regardless of where they are practised: China, the US or Africa.

Why and how can South Africa, as the chair of the AU, African diplomats in Beijing and, most importantly, the Chinese government itself, respond swiftly to those unfortunate events?

The Chinese Foreign Ministry's spokesperson, Zhao Lijian, said: 'We reject differential treatment, and we have zero tolerance for discrimination. Our African friends can count on a fair, just, cordial and friendly reception in China. The foreign ministry will stay in close communication with the Guangdong authorities and continue responding to the African side's reasonable concerns and legitimate appeals.'

Although those are reassuring words, the test of the pudding is in the eating. The current relations between Africa and China, which are effectively conducted and managed through the Forum on China-Africa Cooperation, remain a better mechanism for resolving this kind of diplomatic tension. Why?

Unlike many interstate relations in global affairs, Africa-China relations were firmly established on an anti-racism platform. Hence, acts of racism, whether meted to Africans in China or Chinese in Africa, pose an existential threat to the thriving, strong bond between Africa and China.

It was at the Bandung Conference of 1955 that Africa's relationship with Asian countries, including China, was resolutely affirmed to search for common interests. Having been excluded and marginalised by the US and other developed countries in much of the post-1945 world order, Africans and Asians sought to unite in their study of social, economic and cultural problems, and questions of national sovereignty, racism and colonialism.

It's important to note that as Africans and Chinese now try to speed up the resolution of allegations of racism in China, many of the Bandung Conference demands have not yet been met. Oddly, the current diplomatic tensions between Africa and China come at a time when relations are bearing tangible results on so many fronts. Although trade was adversely affected by the global financial crisis of 2008, the total value of Chinese investment and construction in Africa is close to US$2 trillion since 2005, according to the American Enterprise Institute.

Africa is an important continent for China, especially at this juncture, when its citizens and companies such as Huawei are unfairly treated in the US and some other developed countries. China remains an alternative source of much-needed development finance for Africa.

Increasingly, China is becoming a reliable partner in myriad issues affecting Africa, from Ebola and Covid-19 to security and technology.

It is Africa that supported China's successful claim as a legitimate permanent member of the UN Security Council in 1971, to the detriment of Taiwan. The same was the case for China winning the bid to host the 2008 Olympic Games.

There's an urgent need for China to enforce stringent health measures in response to the war against Covid-19, but that should not be done in a manner in which people are singularly targeted and policed based on their skin colour and appearance.

Of equal importance, Africans in China and Chinese in Africa must abide by the laws of their host countries. The two parties must agree on the need to isolate law-abiding individuals, whether Africans or Chinese, from those involved in acts of criminality in their respective countries.

Covid-19 is colour blind, but world isn't

The term 'colour line', initially used by Frederick Douglass in his essay published in *North American Review*, three years before the Berlin Conference of 1884–1885, captured the racial segregation in the US, vividly. However, W. E. B. Du Bois widened the scope of the term in international relations.

As a leading pan-African scholar and activist who settled in the first independent African country, Ghana, in 1957, Du Bois stated in his book *The Souls of Black Folk* that: 'The problem of the twentieth century is the problem of the colour-line.'

No doubt, the prevailing Covid-19 will profoundly redefine and reshape global politics.

Despite tangible political and economic achievements made in Africa and many parts of the world to roll back racism, Covid-19 has the potential to reinforce the colour lines of the nineteenth and twentieth centuries, as defined by Douglass and Du Bois. There is no scientific proof that Covid-19 as a disease targets Black people. The overwhelming evidence clearly shows that it is indeed colour blind. It targets all people from all races.

However, early signs in the US, Europe and Latin America show that people of African descent are disproportionately affected more than others by the disease. An article in *The New Yorker*, 'Black Plague' by Keeanga-Yamahtta Taylor, stated: 'Thousands of white Americans have also died from the virus, but the pace at which African-Americans are dying has transformed this public-health crisis into an object lesson in racial and class inequality.' At face value, it appears as if this is an American story. It is not.

Globally, Covid-19 will equally have its own colour line. As the poorest and least developed continent, Africa also stands to be disproportionately affected by the pandemic, whether it spreads on the continent as expected or not.

Covid-19 broke out in China late last year when Ghana was granting 126 African-Americans and Afro-Caribbeans citizenship.

To mark the occasion, Ghanaian President Nana Akufo-Addo said: 'We recognise our unique position as the location for 75 per cent of the slave dungeons built on the West Coast of Africa through which the slaves were transported. That is why we had a responsibility to extend the hand of welcome back home to Africans in the diaspora.'

The post-Covid-19 world order will adversely affect Africa. Therefore, Africans must be vigilant and active in reshaping the rules of engagement after the time of Corona. The starting point should be to double their efforts limiting the spread of the pandemic. That should be done concurrently with improvements in public health, safeguarding food security and ensuring that Africa and Africans in the diaspora are at the forefront of the research in finding vaccines for Covid-19.

As it stands, Africa is too fragmented to allow individual countries to marshal effective Covid-19 measures and participate meaningfully in the remaking of the post-Covid-19 global order. The AU should devise a multi-prolonged strategy to re-engage partners in the Global North and South. Most essential in such discussions would be to find ways of handling Africa's debts owed to multilateral institutions and countries and to ensure that that debt is either rescheduled or forgiven, which would allow debt payments to be redirected to the war on Covid-19.

If Africa fails to devise strategies to mitigate the Covid-19 impact, the continent may come out of the pandemic weaker than other continents.

The only way of overcoming the colour line for Africa and Africans in the diaspora is if their social and economic conditions drastically improve. The colour line that began on the plantations in the US appears here to stay.

Cuba a shining light in fight against Coronavirus

On the eve of its 26th Freedom Day, South Africa welcomed a different kind of guest compared to the 2013 Gupta Waterkloof landing.

A team of 217 Cuban medical experts carrying two precious national assets – their national flag and a framed photo of Fidel Castro – landed at Waterkloof Air Force Base in Pretoria. That special visit happened against the backdrop of three notable global developments: the Covid-19 pandemic, fragmentation of the institutions of global governance, and continued sanctions against Cuba by Washington.

It is important to note that Cuba is a tiny island country with a population of 11.4 million. However, it has contributed more medical doctors than all of the G7 countries combined to fight Covid 19. To counter Cuba's noble global efforts to wage war against Covid-19, Washington is leading a campaign to undermine those efforts. Cuban doctors are labelled 'slaves' and 'agents of socialism'.

There have been concerted efforts by right-wing governments close to Washington to send Cuban doctors home: Brazil, Ecuador and Bolivia are examples. When the Brazilian government expelled Cuban doctors in 2018, it alleged that they each cost US$3,100 a month, with 70 per cent of that going to the Cuban government.

Although Cuban doctors were welcomed wholeheartedly in South Africa, there were also efforts to project Cuba as an undemocratic country and one behaving in a massive violation of human rights.

The Cuban medical brigades have been dispatched to Wuhan City in China, Italy's hardest-hit area of Andorra and many countries in Latin America, Europe and Africa.

That selfless action taken by the Cuban government derives from its deep conviction that a successful society requires universal education and health services, compared to a failing health-care system in many developed countries, particularly the US.

In a recent tweet, Josefina Vidal, Cuba's Ambassador to Canada, said: 'Shame on you. Instead of attacking Cuba and its committed doctors, you should be caring about the thousands of sick Americans who are suffering due to the scandalous neglect of your government and the inability of your failed health system to care for them.'

While Cuba leads a global war against Covid-19, the US is undermining the effort by withholding its financial contribution to the World Health Organization.

Instead of leading the world in the fight against Covid-19, the US has been accused of 'modern piracy' for confiscating 200,000 US-made masks in Bangkok that were bound for Germany.

When a British cruise ship with five confirmed Covid-19 cases was denied the right to dock in the US and other ports, Cuba allowed it to dock near Havana. United States President Donald Trump recently defied expert advice by suggesting that people infected by the coronavirus should be injected with toxic disinfectant.

Since the inception of Fidel Castro's revolutionary movement in 1959, Cuba has endured ongoing sabotage, sanctions and economic blockage from the US.

A free health-care system has been a pillar of Cuba's successful revolution. The medical team who arrived at Waterkloof Air Force Base evoked nostalgic dreams deferred for many people.

They came at a time when the revolutionary lexicon of solidarity, free health care and education was being replaced by corruption, cronyism and state capture. The Cuban state was captured to provide health care to all, while the post-apartheid state was captured to liberate mainly the elite.

More importantly, Cuba teaches the world that medical personnel are worth more than sophisticated weaponry.

Africa's place in the global fight for technological dominance

At the 2012 China Initiative Conference organised by the Center for Strategic and International Studies, US Attorney-General William Barr correctly noted that the world is 'now in a new era of global tension and competition'.

China and the US are embroiled in anxiety reminiscent of the Cold War hostility between the US and the Soviet Union.

A US strategic report on China notes that at the inception of formal US-China relations in 1979, the US hoped that recognising China 'would spur fundamental economic and political opening in the PRC (People's Republic of China) and lead to its emergence as a constructive and responsible global stakeholder with a more open society'.

However, the report ruefully notes that that hope has been dashed. It alleges that China has not exported its economic reforms to other dimensions of its society in terms of political liberties and other forms of expression that are typical of liberal societies.

Sino-American tension has become even more pronounced during the Trump administration in the US. Once again, Africa will be forced, in subtle ways, to pick sides – just like it was during the Cold War. One of the most fractious issues igniting the tension that Barr talked about is technological dominance. Controlling 5G networks in the twenty-first century is a massive issue for ambitious global players such as China and the US.

Huawei, a Chinese technological giant, has been a centre of attention and an object of suspicion in the US. Africa has recently been more inclined to cultivating closer economic and technological relations with China than the US, which has not gone unnoticed by that country.

Naturally, the US has been overt in its discomfort with China's seeming success with Africa.

The US has justified its misgivings about Huawei by arguing that the tech giant might be China's agent for global espionage. Africa is a growing consumer of technology and needs it to tackle the challenges of virtual isolation against the rest of the world. Huawei has established itself across Africa and, predictably, the US has been loathsome about that, while China has been emphatic in its opposition to US animosity.

Like the United States, China also realises the enormous potential in Africa, not only as a consumer of technology but also as an arena for players with ambitions of global dominance.

Africa finds itself in an invidious position. Its history has mainly been shaped by its multifaceted relationship with the West. However, that history was also an incentive for Africa and China to establish close ties to end colonial domination.

Recently, Africa and China have become closer in their economic ties. While that is happening, Africa has remained close in its political and social outlook with the West.

The circumstances summon the need for agile diplomacy. Historically, non-African players have treated Africa with condescension, dictating how it should conduct its affairs and with whom.

In *China's Second Continent* (Knopf, 2014), American journalist and academic Howard French narrates that, in the twenty-first century, Africa is still being treated like a 'baby', a continent that is incapable of offering political, intellectual and economic import to the international system. That attitude explains non-African intentions of evangelising to Africa.

Nelson Mandela offered a strong response to non-African attitudes of patronising Africa. In 1990, he was asked about his praise for divisive leaders such as Yasser Arafat, Fidel Castro and Muammar Gaddafi and how his cosy relationship with them raised the eyebrows of those who expected him to be a paragon of human rights globally.

Mandela responded that the problem with political punditry, mainly of Western provenance, is that it is undergirded by the attitude that whomever the West considers its enemy should be Africa's enemy, too.

He went on to say that the relationship of South Africa's ANC with other global players was shaped by the attitude of those actors towards the ANC. In essence, Mandela was arguing that the ANC had a close relationship with those who helped its crusade against apartheid.

The West was occasionally equivocal in denouncing apartheid and calling for democracy in South Africa, fearing that the ANC would establish a communist government.

The ANC never forgot that, and in Mandela's interview, again in the US with Robert MacNeil, Mandela reminded him that shortly after its proscription, the ANC and its leaders in exile had sought American help. Their supplications were rejected, forcing the ANC to seek the succour of African governments and the support of players such as the Soviet Union. Mandela's assertions appear somewhat prescient, considering the current circumstances of binary politics.

Africa is the least developed continent in the world and thus should welcome relations that can help to change its impoverished condition.

China has been an attractive partner to Africa, mainly because of its reiteration that Africa is its equal partner. Second, China's unconditional relations with Africa pose a stark contrast to conditions that the West typically demands.

It helps that China was never a coloniser in Africa. From the West, Africa has adopted economic and political ideologies that are more inclined to the market and multiparty politics. Thus, Africa has the responsibility of sifting through the components of its relations with other partners and adopting features that can help the continent.

But Africa should not succumb to the pressure of choosing sides in the tension that now claims attention in global politics. The same applies to the consumption of technology.

If Africa is loath to consume technology from non-African partners, the decision should be Africa's to make, after vigilant deliberations. The US is not helping its case against China when its attitude arguably suggests anxiety about sharing dominance with a non-Western, non-Caucasian power.

Is Huwawei any different to other tech giants, or are we just getting caught up in Trump's mud-slinging?

South African journalist and academic Heidi Swart has drawn an analogy between the Coronavirus and the possibly troubling effect of Huawei in South Africa. Her article in *Daily Maverick* obliquely argues that Huawei is a different kind of virus that could endanger South Africa's cyber-security.

The world has been held captive by the emergence and spread of the Coronavirus for almost the entire first half of 2020. The virus has also emerged at one of the most inauspicious junctures in twenty-first-century politics, one that is characterised by ultra-nationalism in global players like the United States, the United Kingdom, Brazil and India. Nationalists such as Donald Trump in the US and Jair Bolsonaro in Brazil initially wanted to play down the portentous effect of the Coronavirus. While Trump seemed to have at least tempered his initial denialism, Bolsonaro has not yielded to reasonable counsel and scientific opinion.

That backdrop creates some context in which Swart's article 'Are South Africans safe with Huawei? (Part Two): A Different Kind of Virus' can be understood. Swart argues that Huawei poses a great risk to South Africa because the country does not have mechanisms such as the UK's Huawei Cyber Security Evaluation Centre, which is a leader in advising the UK government on cyber-security. Swart laments the fact that South Africa does not have such a body, despite it being more exposed to Huawei than the UK.

South Africa's State Security Agency (SSA) is never subjected to vigorous parliamentary scrutiny, and its responses to concerns over cyber-security seem to be woefully inadequate and exasperatingly vague. The Joint Standing Committee on Intelligence (JSCI) does not help to demystify the SSA's activities and capabilities, as meetings are usually closed to the public. Swart might be forgiven for not familiarising herself with the workings of parliamentary committees on intelligence matters across the world. The JSCI operates like all democratic parliament committees, including those in the UK and the US, holding meetings about extremely sensitive matters of national security behind closed doors.

The security breaches and lapses that were exposed under Siyabonga Cwele's tenure as Minister of State Security have continued under the incumbent, Ayanda Dlodlo. South Africa's vulnerability to cyber espionage and its alarmingly high levels of crime and doubtful efficiency of the South African Police Service justify the intent of articles such as Swart's.

However, Swart's article is an addition to the anti-China narrative that is arguably successful in Western politics and traffics mostly in underscoring the possible threats that Huawei's technological advances herald. Through the Federal Communications Commission, the United States bans carriers in rural America from tapping the Universal Service Fund to purchase Huawei equipment, with the Senate voting unanimously to replace it, along with that of ZTE. Five Chinese entities were added to the 2019 US Entity List for 'acting contrary to the national security or foreign policy interests of the United States'.

More than security concerns, what seems to be playing out in the mudslinging between the Trump administration and Huawei is American unwillingness to risk competition for 5G prominence with a Chinese entity. That is a tussle between the two governments (American and Chinese) with Huawei conflated with the Chinese government. It is noteworthy that the United Kingdom has had to backtrack on engaging Huawei services because of Conservative Party concerns and America's animosity to its closest ally enlisting the services of a tech giant emanating from one of America's mortal rivals.

From that backdrop, even though Swart's article offers nothing new, it joins a general trend of Western antipathy towards China's technological advances. Washington has been the leading campaigner of that anti-China narrative.

Should South Africa be caught up in that jostling? The correct answer is that South Africa should be leery of actors who are involved in its security status. That should be applied to all actors, both from the West and the rest. Swart conspicuously leaves out the security concerns that come with Western tech giants such as Facebook, Twitter and the defunct Cambridge Analytica who have been accused of similar allegations levelled against Huawei.

Furthermore, Facebook and Twitter have lent themselves to polarising political narratives, especially in the United States, which are likely to shape political events in the US and beyond. It is also noteworthy that Facebook has been especially notorious in harvesting and storing data from users across the world. When one talks about Huawei's perceived intent, such conduct by non-Chinese tech giants should also be mentioned, which makes the argument that vigilance should be applied to all tech giants more compelling.

But Swart's article is a timely cautionary tale because fears of Huawei working at the behest of the Chinese government are understandable, notwithstanding their arguable veracity. However, articles that seek to raise concerns about Huawei would be more rigorous if they provided the context in which Huawei is characterised as a concern.

Second, such opinion should also take cognisance of cyber threats that have hitherto been conducted by entities other than the Chinese.

Third, South Africa should be presumed to be a sovereign country with rights to decide whom it wants to engage.

Fourth, there is a political history to Sino-South African trust that influences South Africa's seeming confidence in China and its multinational corporations. In a world of rational agents, national identities, interests and conduct are shaped by a confluence of historical, cultural, social, economic and political factors. Those, in turn, influence the presumed or inferred interests in the relations that nations establish.

Historically, China has presented itself to South Africa as a non-interfering, well-meaning partner. At the same time, the United States was historically sympathetic to capitalist politics, even in their most vulgar and racist guise. That was because the capitalist West was poised to work with any player who disavowed the non-capitalist players.

With China having replaced the Soviet Union, the acrimonious dichotomy between the US and the Soviet Union during the Cold War seems to be playing itself out to this day. As was the case then, Western intentions over Africa should be scrutinised because they may not necessarily be for Africa's benefit: they could be gambits used to curtail the influence of America's perceived foes. As South Africa appraises the pros and cons of engaging Huawei, it should keep those eventualities in mind.

While Swart rightly decries South Africa's incapacity to repel cyber threats, she should nonetheless avoid targeting Huawei. All possible threats should be targeted, irrespective of their provenance.

In the final analysis, it will be South Africa's prerogative to elect whom it enlists for its 5G ambitions. What is certain now is that the United States is not doing itself favours by pandering to ultra-nationalism, racial denialism and humouring a president who cannot be counted upon as a reasonable voice in international affairs. China and enterprises that emanate from there could gain a lot of sympathy by being more level-headed than the United States.

Swart's analogies between the Coronavirus and Huawei's activities in South Africa are also a curious venture because it purports not to see any positive thing in Huawei's advance. And because the article has not been supported by unimpeachable evidence that Huawei spies on South Africa, the virus analogy is unfortunate.

Hong Kong internal crisis needs attention

Why is it hard for Britain and the US to garner sufficient global support on the Hong Kong question?

Put simply, countries in the Global South, especially the African countries, find it difficult to align themselves with the China containment strategy guised in democratic language.

First, Hongkongers cannot be denied their democratic right to express their legitimate concerns over issues that affect how they are governed. The challenge for those expressing their democratic right to be heard through demonstrations is mainly on the tactics to be employed to achieve their objectives.

The lesson learned from the crisis in Zimbabwe, a country that shares historical similarities with Hong Kong, is the need to resolve internal political challenges with less interference from the colonial power, Britain.

In 1842, China's Qing Dynasty realised the corrosive impact of opium on its people. It instructed its senior official, Lin Zexu, at Canton Harbour (Hong Kong) to blockade the shipping of the drug into the country.

In her book titled *The Opium War* (Picador, 2011), Julia Lovell compellingly argued that the British invaded China as a move to 'open up a closed, xenophobic empire to the outside world'.

Similarly, the British, represented by Cecil John Rhodes, shredded a non-aggression treaty Queen Victoria signed with King Lobengula in 1888 and lynched the king of the Ndebele people in 1887 and later publicly hanged the spiritual leader of the Shona people, Mbuya Nehanda.

The current crisis in Hong Kong is largely perceived to be a colonial and hegemonic hangover. There have been numerous moves led by the US to contain the rise of China in recent years. In a closer look at the events in Hong Kong and how they play out in US electoral politics, it appears that Hong Kong is increasingly becoming a major point of the emerging 'New Cold War' likened to the situation in Berlin after World War 2.

As was the case during the Cold War, Africa is poised to lose in the tensions in the South China Sea and, particularly, Hong Kong. Africa and the Global South are driven by the fact that Hong Kong is a special administrative region of the People's Republic of China.

While sympathetic to the legitimate concerns of Hongkongers, it is critical that the internal political crisis in Hong Kong is resolved without the involvement of colonial and imperialist powers. Hong Kong remains an important trading hub for Africa and the world.

China-India border face-off has worrying global impact, not least for Africa and Brics

The current breakdown in relations between China and India has far-reaching implications for the world and solidarity in the developing world. Expectedly, border misunderstanding in the disputed Line of Actual Control has been the accelerant for the current situation.

The recent clash that claimed the lives of 20 Indian soldiers was the deadliest in more than 40 years, and the situation is growing more tense. According to *The Sydney Morning Herald*, 'satellite images released by Maxar, a Colorado-based satellite imagery company, shows the new construction along the Galwan River Valley occurring against a backdrop of worsening relations between the two countries.'

India-China disputes in that region are longstanding. It is noteworthy that the Sino-Indian principles of peaceful coexistence that were signed in 1954 between China's Zhou Enlai and India's Jawaharlal Nehru were partly aimed at fortifying good neighbourliness between the two countries, thus avoiding disputes like the current one. The border war of 1962 threatened that peaceful coexistence and the recent resurgence of that dispute shows that the peace that followed the 1962 war was delicate.

With hindsight, the resurgence of the India-China border disputes seems to have been almost inevitable. Since Xi Jinping came to power in 2013, he has steered China in a more assertive direction and has emboldened the country not to be bashful about its achievements and potential. His China Dream concept is an oblique signal to the US that China will continue its path to economic and military strength, which will unavoidably dent America's global domination.

Between 2009 and 2018, military spending in China rose by 83%, which is part of Xi's intent to make China's army world-class by mid-century and to put together an army that can fight and win wars. Diplomatically, Xi has been active in courting the developing world, and the West too, through enterprises such as the Belt and Road Initiative. His utterances demonstrate faith in a multilateral international order.

India seems to be drifting in the opposite direction since Narendra Modi took the helm of the country. Amid Sino-American disputes, India has blatantly taken America's side. That does not bode well for the future of the developing world.

There are several reasons why the current Sino-Indian dispute could have global implications that are infinitely more considerable than those of former conflicts. First is the fact that China is now the world's second-biggest economy with an increasingly modernising army.

Second, with 1.43 billion and 1.37 billion people in China and India, respectively, the two countries constitute 37 per cent of the global population. For that reason, whatever happens between them will engulf a considerable fraction of the world in turmoil.

Third, the world is currently destabilised by Covid-19, and China and India should play a central role in curbing the virus. The virus originated in China, and doubts notwithstanding, China has reasonably tried to contain it. India is a seminal player in the export of medical supplies. According to *export.gov*, 'the Indian healthcare industry amounted to US$150 billion in 2018 and is expected to reach US$280 billion by 2022 due to the increased demand for specialised and quality healthcare facilities.'

Thus, the synergy between China and India could be crucial in containing the spread of Covid-19. Another reason why the stakes are high in Sino-Indian relations is that the two countries are the leading powers of the developing world. Hence, the implications of their interactions impinge on the rest of the developing world, which is where the case of Africa comes in.

Africa's relationship with China and India was formalised at the celebrated Bandung Conference in Indonesia in 1955. That conference was a bedrock of the developing world's concerted struggle against imperialism. It was also a prelude to initiatives such as the Non-Aligned Movement (NAM).

Historically, both China and India looked askance at the capitalist West, a scepticism induced by an intersecting discomfort with capitalism and the racial stratification by the West that had caused the suppression of people of colour in the developing world. In that respect, Africa was a natural kindred spirit of China and India.

The current nationalistic sentiment that is seeping into countries such as the US and the UK evokes memories of the colonial order. It is thus troubling that India seems to be joining that resurgence of nationalism, which carries with it religious chauvinism, racial strife, anti-immigrant sentiment and withdrawal from multilateralism.

Furthermore, India's ban of 59 apps from China is understandable, even though it confirms that India is espousing a hostile attitude towards China that has been Donald Trump's playbook from his 2016 campaign to date. And all that goes against the aspirations of the developing world.

The Brazil, Russia, India, China and South Africa group of countries represents the premium body for amplifying the voice of the developing world on the global stage. Since 2014, Russia and Brazil have suffered economically, South Africa's economy has taken a hit, China's growth has also been slowing down, while India's has been unsteady. However, the two countries enjoy a clear advantage over the remaining three members of Brics.

Brazil, under Jair Bolsonaro, like India, has overtly shown that its sympathies are with the US rather than China. Thus, within Brics, Africa could only count on Russia, China and South Africa to maintain a commitment towards staunching the crises besetting the region. That does not augur well, especially considering the massive strain that Covid-19 has exacted on Russia and South Africa. Prospects in the near future illustrate that Africa might not have respite anytime soon. Trump will use the same formula that helped him to get elected in 2016, which is the formula that Modi has used, as shown through his government's suppression of the Muslim population.

From the look of things, Africa is more likely to move towards China, especially in the sphere of economics. At the same time, India will most likely seek to benefit economically from Sino-American trade disputes. That scenario is not ideal because Africa's situation is such that it should create beneficial relations with powers that can help to improve the continent's lot. That depends on a robust concerted voice from the developing world, which would carry a lot of weight if endorsed by power players such as China and India.

Alas, the current Sino-Indian dispute occludes that from happening.

Tensions between Africa's greatest allies must be resolved peacefully

Two significant events related to China and India have placed the Global South, in general, and Africa, in particular, in a predicament.

In mid-June, those two countries were involved in a bloody clash leaving 20 Indian soldiers dead and an unknown number on the Chinese side in Galwan Valley alongside the disputed border.

In an unprecedented move, India this week banned 59 popular Chinese mobile apps including TikTok, WeChat, UC Browser, Shareit and Baidu Map. If unresolved, the worsening tensions will make an irreparable dent in the Global South's quest for the transformation of the institutions of global governance.

More importantly, those tensions have the potential to reverse the economic gains made in Beijing and New Delhi. Although it remains unlikely, the conflict between those nuclear powers stands to destabilise global peace and security. Africa and the rest of the Global South find it hard to take sides, as Beijing and New Delhi are important allies.

At this juncture, Washington appears to be the main beneficiary of the conflict. Since Barack Obama's pivot to Asia, Washington has been drawing New Delhi to its side in a move to limit China's rise.

In recent times, Washington has been moving military hardware near China in the South China Sea. It has furthermore intensified a trade war, selling arms to Taiwan and interfering in Hong Kong, Tibet and the Xinjiang province. As it stands, Beijing is under siege, as Washington's hand appears in almost all issues it faces with its neighbours. In such a situation, minor border skirmishes, such as the one in the Galwan Valley, could lead to miscalculations on both sides, ending in a war.

India's Prime Minister, Narendra Modi, like US President Donald Trump, has diverted global attention from his mismanagement of the Coronavirus pandemic and the ill-treatment of the Muslim minority by focusing the nation on China.

There is an ill-conceived idea in New Delhi that India will benefit from the current tensions between Washington and Beijing. It is expected that global companies will relocate from China to India in the wake of the trade war and the coronavirus pandemic.

Although liberal democracy gives India an advantage over other countries in the region to become a hub in the value chain, Vietnam, a communist country, appears to be the most preferred country by those companies.

What will be the implications of those tensions for Brics and Africa?

Since the Bandung Conference of 1955, China and India have played a critical role in the fight against colonialism and apartheid. As the largest developing countries (with more than 1 billion people each), China and India rallied the Global South in demanding the transformation of the post-World War 2 world order.

India's pivot to the Quadrilateral Security Dialogue (US, Japan, Australia, India) and the Global North Alliance will fundamentally dilute Brics and significantly weaken its ability to push for a change in the current global order. As China and India constitute a large portion of Africa's trade, tensions between Africa's greatest allies should and must be resolved peacefully.

US health secretary's visit to Taiwan crosses red line

In his influential book, *On China* (Penguin, 2011), former United States Secretary of State and National Security Advisor Henry Kissinger narrates an encounter he had with China's Premier Zhou Enlai during which Kissinger described China as a mysterious place with mysterious people. Zhou queried what that meant, even though the implication was clear: for centuries, China was an enigma to the outside, and even after the accession of the Chinese Communist Party to power in 1949, the country remained mostly closed to the outside world.

That wilful self-isolation hurt China's international image because it allowed foreign observers to form and promote impressions of China that were not always palatable. Since Deng Xiaoping started reforms in 1978, China has been opening up to the rest of the world in multiple ways. Those range from membership of multilateral organisations, invitations of foreign direct investment, international party-to-party relations, and China's going-out policies, which have seen an exponential increase in China's presence through multinational organisations, non-state entrepreneurship and tourism outside of China.

That growing visibility has had mixed consequences for China and the burgeoning number of its partners and detractors. To its enthusiastic partners in the developing world, China's increasing influence on global affairs and economics provides a model for how developing countries could be prosperous without following liberal-democratic dogma.

To its detractors, China's increasing influence and preponderance on global affairs threaten the status quo, which has mostly favoured Western players. Central to those circumstances and perceptions is the importance of diplomacy and messaging, which should mostly be China's responsibility.

While commemorating the 40th anniversary of the 'Message to Compatriots in Taiwan' at the Great Hall of the People on 2 January last year, President Xi Jinping said, 'China must be on guard against "black swan" risk while fending off "grey rhino". Black swan refers to 'unpredictable events' while grey rhino is a 'highly probable, high-impact yet neglected threat'.

In the coming few days, top Chinese Communist Party (CCP) leaders will meet at Beidaihe for their annual retreat to critically assess prevailing domestic, regional and international events. There are numerous issues that the Chinese leadership could ponder on at that critical gathering, ranging from Covid-19 and its impact on the economy; divesting floods in Jiujiang; trade war with the US; Hong Kong; Taiwan; the border dispute with India and the worsening tension with the US.

At this particular juncture, China can best be described as a country under siege, similar to the early phase of the Chinese Communist Revolution. The US and a few developed countries such as the UK and Australia have mounted an unprecedented frontal diplomatic, economic and ideological assault against China. The attacks on Huawei and TikTok are examples of things to come.

The visit to Taiwan of US Health Secretary Alex M. Azar II has ultimately crossed the red line. It no doubt opens the possibility of a forceful unification of China not just with Hong Kong but also the renegade territory of Taiwan.

In other words, the US's provocative moves in Taiwan might be the catalyst in making Taiwan a perfect centenary gift for President Xi Jinping and the CCP leadership next year.

Biden-Harris ticket and US China policy

The first joint appearance of Kamala Harris as the presumptive Democratic nominee alongside Joe Biden sent clear signals that President Donald Trump's days in the White House are numbered.

It is also important to note the significance of Harris's appointment to that position as the first woman with African and Indian heritage. However, lessons learnt from the Obama presidency are that one's background carries little influence in the making of foreign policy.

What would be Biden-Harris foreign policy towards the rest of the world? What is Biden's China policy, and how could it affect Africa?

The US and China are major players in Africa; hence, their relations on global issues such as trade, climate change, peace and security significantly impact Africa.

Biden's immediate task as president would be handling the three most critical domestic issues, namely: the Covid-19 pandemic, the economy and race relations.

However, there is likely to be change and continuity within Washington's China policy. Biden's engagements with China would be shredding Trump's allegation that Biden is 'soft on China'. As someone who served on the Senate foreign relations committee as well as vice president under Obama, Biden is more familiar with China and Africa.

During the Democratic presidential primaries, Biden and Harris were critical of China. Biden labelled President Xi Jinping a 'thug'. He also referred to China as eating 'our lunch'.

Once settled in the White House, Biden would probably abandon Trump's all-out antagonistic approach towards China.

Among Biden's advisory team are Susan Rice, Samantha Power and Anne-Marie Slaughter, whose views on foreign policy favour multilateralism over unilateralism.

It is unlikely that Washington's relations with Beijing could go back to the glory years of Clinton, Bush and Obama. The team would rekindle America's relationship with its Western partners in resuscitating a liberal international order.

Henceforth, Washington under Biden-Harris would probably return to the Paris Agreement, the Joint Comprehensive Plan of Action with Iran, and numerous UN agencies, especially the World Health Organization. To succeed, Biden will require China's cooperation and support.

There will be continued heightened tension with China in the South China Sea, Hong Kong, Taiwan and in the competition for dominance in the roll-out of 5G and other technologies.

Although tension with China will continue, Washington won't behave like a lone ranger as Trump did during his disastrous years in the White House. The cooperation between Washington and Beijing within multilateral forums bodes well for Africa. As the least-developed continent, Africa's development largely depends on a peaceful global order.

The Covid-19 pandemic and climate issues are demanding the attention of the world's biggest economies.

To achieve Agenda 2063, Africa will need cooperation and support from the US and China, and that should be Africa's expectation from the incoming Biden-Harris administration.

India, China and Africa: A delicate balancing act in the reign of Narendra Modi

Africa has a history with India that is deep and multifaceted. Untold numbers of Indians were brought to South Africa for indentured servitude. Over time, many Indians were ensconced in other African nations. They became integral to the African social fabric, and many people of Indian descent have gone on to hold influential positions in their African countries.

Mahatma Gandhi spent some of his formative political time in South Africa. It was here that he was subjected to some of the racism that spurred the anti-racist and anti-colonial crusade that defined the rest of his life. That also inspired the fledgeling nationalist sentiment in Africa. Even though Gandhi's legacy, especially as it concerns his views on Black Africans, is being challenged, he held beliefs and opinions that were consonant with the African struggle against racist and colonial oppression.

Shortly after its independence from Britain, India had a natural affinity to other survivors of colonial rule. Its foreign policy was thus decidedly anti-imperialist and tilted towards forging synergy in the developing world. Jawaharlal Nehru, the first prime minister, was at the centre of India's original foreign policy. In 1954, he signed the five principles of peaceful coexistence with China's Zhou Enlai. The following year, at the Bandung Conference in Indonesia, India and China promoted the five principles of peaceful coexistence and succeeded in having them affirmed as the principles for peace in the developing world.

Five more principles were added at the Conference to make them ten. Since then, India's image in the developing world has been one of a kindred spirit. The conference also paved the way for the establishment of the Non-Aligned Movement, which was the biggest demonstration to date of Afro-Asian solidarity.

Historically in international affairs, India would take the non-aligned stance that Africa favoured. Africa and India's quest was to change the lopsided structure of the global system that was tilted in favour of the West and erstwhile colonisers. India is part of the Group of 77 from which it augmented its role in improving the lot of the developing world.

More recently, India's commitment to the developing world is demonstrated through the Brazil, Russia, India, China and South Africa group of countries. However, since the accession of Narendra Modi to the premiership, India's priorities and sympathies are changing, and the change is so apparent that it might alter Africa's and the entire Global South's perceptions of progressive India.

Modi is more nationalistic in his politics. His government has had a controversial relationship with Indian Muslims, and there are charges that Hindu extremism is being excused if not actively encouraged by the government to the detriment of Muslim citizens. That seems to bode well for the current US government whose draconian attitude towards predominantly Muslim countries is well known. Thus, it is not surprising that Modi and Donald Trump have a close relationship. With a large Muslim population, Africa will find it hard to embrace what appears to be India's emerging state intolerance of Muslims.

India joined the Quadrilateral Security Dialogue (Quad), a forum between the US, Australia and Japan. It is evident that India is unsettled by China's security ambitions and so joining Quad is calculated towards keeping China in check.

India and China have been locked in a border dispute, which does not augur well for solidarity in the developing world. At the time of Bandung, India and China were influential champions of the developing world. Currently, with their much-improved economic status and political influence, coupled with vast populations, India and China are strategically placed to push the just inclusion of the developing world in the mainstream global economic system. While India's legitimate right to defend its sovereignty is fully understood, drifting away from Brics into the camp of the US (Quad) at the expense of Africa and the Global South will come at a high cost.

India's close relationship with the US under current nationalistic sentiment could mean that it will continually drift away from its commitment to the developing world, which has profound implications for India and the developing countries. It means that in the Arab-Israeli conflict, for example, India will take Israel's side to appease the US and domestically appease its anti-Muslim citizens, which might put India at odds with its African partners.

That dissonance might, in turn, disrupt other dimensions of Afro-Indian relations.

Africa has been generous in giving India opportunities to sell its technologies and medicines. India is currently one of the top three trade partners of sub-Saharan Africa. Although it cannot compete with China in Africa, there are several ways through which India can leverage its presence there. One way is to work its diaspora in Africa. Another is encouraging Africa to amplify its voice on international matters. Understandably, India could do all of that while pursuing its interests. However, following its interests need not be a zero-sum game between India and its partners – Africa in this case.

The India-Africa Forum Summit is something that India could use to improve its relationship with Africa. At the 2015 Summit, about 40 African heads of state attended, signalling the importance they attach to India. That happened before Trump became US president. India and Africa noted that, even though between them they constitute nearly one-third of humanity, they continue to be excluded from appropriate representation in the institutions of global governance that were designed for an era long since past.

At the 2015 Summit, India committed a concessional Line of Credit of US$10 billion and US$600 million in grant assistance. On average, over 8,000 African youth are trained in a range of programmes in India annually, and Indian companies have invested over US$54 billion in Africa. By 2018, India's trade with Africa was more than US$62 billion.

That shows that, despite Modi's tilt towards the West, India still has what could amount to a coherent policy towards Africa. However, India could enhance its reputation even further if it mends fences with China and takes meaningful strides to shatter allegations that it is growing increasingly anti-Muslim and nationalistic.

Daily Maverick / Opinionista / 7 September 2020

Four more years of Donald Trump bodes ill for the future of Africa

The Trump Administration has taken a dismissive and patronising approach to Africa, including Trump describing the continent in very insulting and derogatory ways, calling some African countries 'shitholes'. However, if the US wants to maintain its place at the pinnacle of the global pecking order, it needs Africa.

The 2020 United States presidential election is crucial and consequential for many reasons, ranging from its domestic issues such as race and the economy to international issues such as its moral and political standing and influence in the world.

The Donald Trump administration has lived up to the expectations and fears that Trump represented during his eccentric 2016 campaign. He has inflamed racial sentiment in domestic affairs, embraced conspiracy theorists who support him, and withdrawn the US from international treaties and agreements that he thought were to the country's detriment. He has also upped the ante in attacking China, the country that poses the greatest threat to the US's enduring standing as the most influential global power.

The Coronavirus pandemic, which Trump calls 'the China virus', has added another complication to global politics and China-America rivalry, in particular. The US's handling of the pandemic has been stunningly ineffectual and, to deflect the backlash, Trump has had to blame Democrats and some specialists within the US and, of course, China at the international level. Indeed, the Sino-US rivalry has conjured up the spectre of a new Cold War.

The prospect of an emerging Cold War has global consequences because it means that the rest of the world will be compelled to pick on which side their sympathies lie. That is likely to have significant implications for Africa, a continent that needs strong relations with the more developed regions of the world. Africa is also susceptible to superpower hectoring because of its weak economic situation and attendant lesser influence on global affairs.

Unfortunately, the Trump Administration has taken a patronising and dismissive approach to Africa. Africa could scarcely forget how Trump described it in insulting and derogatory ways. However, if the US wants to maintain its place at the pinnacle of the global pecking order, it needs Africa. Africa is the youngest continent with almost 60 per cent of the population under the age of 25, and its population is set to grow exponentially in the next 50 years. The US appreciates that, even though Trump's actions might suggest otherwise. The fight against global terrorism, which has been a vital preoccupation of the US since 2001, can be assured of success only if Africa is brought to its centre. A lack of development in Africa creates a conducive environment for disgruntled citizens to gravitate towards extremist groups that rebel against ineffectual and corrupt governments.

Also, mobilisation towards terrorist groups might escalate in Africa because the young population will continue to grow, adding more potential converts, especially if Africa does not manage to provide sufficient employment and economic opportunities. For that reason, the US will need to work closely with countries where terrorist groups have been the most active: Nigeria, Kenya, Somalia and now Mozambique.

All of that, however, might, to a significant degree, depend on the outcome of the November election in the US. A victory for Trump would mean a continuation, if not worsening, of what has been the case over the past four years. Trump would continue on his current path because another victory would be an affirmation that his methods and views are working and appreciated by voters. That, however, could bode ill for certain parts of American society and many parts of the world, Africa included.

For Africa, the issue of immigration and duress to disengage from China in the political and technological sphere will come to the fore. However, the US will have to show wilful and unmistakable intent to engage with the continent as an important region for future global politics. Emigration has been pivotal to propping up some of Africa's faltering economies. South Sudan, for example, received remittance flows from its emigrants to wealthier foreign countries of US$1.3 billion in 2019, which is about 34 per cent of the country's GDP. Nigeria received by far the largest remittance flows with US$23.8 billion, followed by Ghana (US$3.5 billion) and Kenya (US$2.8 billion).

Those numbers go to the heart of what hostility to emigration could entail. It is inarguable that countries should be vigilant in admitting migrants.

However, vigilance and strictness should not usurp the importance of fairness and humanity in the case of refugees.

The November election is vital to Africa for more reasons than those mentioned above. It could also dictate the political texture of the continent. The Obama Administration tried to be normative in its relations with Africa by urging African governments to adhere to the tenets of democracy and put constitutions and the well-being of citizens before the ambitions of rulers.

That has changed under the Trump Administration, as seen even in the US where some expectations of democracy have been brazenly eroded. Trump has characterised peaceful protesters as terrorists and anarchists, among other unsavoury descriptions. Police brutality has been excused. Trump has gone further to express misgivings about the credibility of America's voting system, which is an indirect hint that should he lose the upcoming election, he might not concede defeat.

What would another four years of Trump mean for Africa? The US-African relationship would likely revert to what it was during the Cold War. The US would establish strong bonds with African leaders who distance themselves from China, irrespective of the democratic credentials of such leaders. That, in turn, would mean that extensions of term limits in Africa would be met with indifference if not encouragement by the US, if those who did so stood by their side.

Despite the bleak possibilities, there are still opportunities for the rejuvenation of Afro-American cooperation. American engagement in other spheres in Africa, ranging from security to non-government advocacy and education, could give the US an advantage over other competitors in Africa. All of that, however, will be significantly influenced by the outcome of the US's 2020 election and the temperament of its next administration.

The race for a Covid-19 vaccine has become the new frontier of US-China competition in Africa

On 6 October 2020, *Nature*, the premier science journal, broke with its tradition of strictly separating science and politics. It argued in an editorial that, 'science and politics have always depended on each other ... At the same time, science and research inform and shape a spectrum of public policies, from environmental protection to data ethics.'

The outbreak and spread of Covid-19 has witnessed the rise of health diplomacy, wherein matters of medical science are increasingly influencing and shaping the conduct of diplomacy as well as the field of international relations. The US and China's geopolitical tug-of-war has intensified lately, entering an arena most sensitive to Africa and the rest of the developing world: health. Africa looks to the US and China as major strategic partners in its quest to find a comprehensive strategy to combat Covid-19.

Shockingly, Washington and Beijing have embraced different approaches, attitudes and strategies towards Covid-19 that appear to be at odds with Africa's needs. The race for a Covid-19 vaccine, in particular, has taken a nationalistic tone at home and geostrategic calculus abroad.

On the home front, the US continues to lack a coherent national strategy to arrest the spread of Coronavirus. Political calculations seem to be driving the approach that the current US administration has assumed. Indeed, the example set by President Donald Trump is baffling and could lull his devout supporters into taking a casual stance on Covid-19. Even leaders who are presumed to be close to Trump, such as the United Kingdom's Boris Johnson, have been strict in imposing stringent measures to stem the spread of the pandemic.

The Republicans in the US are largely silent on Trump's reckless attitude. In recent days, Coronavirus infection figures in the US have reached an alarming 7 million and caused 214,844 deaths. As the country goes to the polls in the next 20 days, the Coronavirus has become one of the major issues that will determine the outcome of elections on 3 November 2020.

Despite having been infected by the virus, President Trump's attitude towards Covid-19, appears irrational and unaware of its impact on the ordinary people in the United States and the world. For Africa, the 214,844 death figure in the US is not just a sheer number. The bulk of those adversely affected by Covid-19 and who end up dying from it are none other than African-Americans whose ancestral roots are deeply anchored in Africa.

Globally, Trump continues to wreak havoc, undermining the post-World War 2 institutions designed to shield the most vulnerable nations from pandemics such as Covid-19. The US abandoned the WHO, a premier global institution that Africa relies upon heavily to combat Covid-19. If that was not enough, the Trump administration has heightened tension with China, turning healthcare matters pertaining to Covid-19 into geopolitical instruments with geo-economic benefits.

China, on the other hand, appears to have arrested the spread of Covid-19 on the home front and is witnessing a gradual resumption of normalcy in its economy. Unlike the US, China embarked upon draconian measures and strict adherence to Covid-19 protocols, which have brought resoundingly positive results through low numbers of infections and deaths. More importantly, China has strengthened its position within the WHO by increasing its funding of the institution. While the US shuns global initiatives such as the Covax facility, China has joined, becoming a major power (Covax is the WHO-led global scheme to ensure fair distribution of Covid-19 vaccines, with 156 countries having joined so far).

Worryingly, Africa, with the largest number of poor countries in the world, has neither the capacity nor the resources to produce its own vaccines or effectively manage the impact of Covid-19. It has, however, tapped into its strategic partners across the world to alleviate the situation. Africa has attracted China's attention, far beyond its extractive industries and infrastructure development. A rising scientific leader in the field of medicine, Beijing entered that competitive arena. In its response to Africa's call for assistance in handling the pandemic, Beijing held a successful China-Africa Extraordinary Summit on Solidarity Against Covid-19 in June 2020.

A recently released World Bank report projected that economies in sub-Saharan Africa would fall by 3.3% due to the Coronavirus. It estimates that 40 million Africans will be forced to live below the poverty line. The African Development Bank was compelled to revise its 2020 Economic Outlook to reflect the dire impact that the Coronavirus will have on Africa. That has prompted President Cyril Ramaphosa as African Union chair to appeal to the world for US$1 billion to alleviate the situation.

President Xi Jinping specifically pledged that 'once the development and deployment of the Covid-19 vaccine is completed in China, African countries will be among the first to benefit'. China has, furthermore, committed to building up Africa's Centres for Disease Control and Prevention. Its close relations with Africa, particularly in healthcare and specifically on the prospective Coronavirus candidate vaccines, have become another arena for conflict with the US. The US signalled its discomfort about what it perceives to be China's encroachment on its sphere of influence.

Meanwhile, Egypt has signed an agreement with China to be the main African centre to distribute prospective Chinese Covid-19 vaccines. That is in line with President Xi's desire to make Chinese Covid-19 vaccines public goods. Equally important, it will be key for China as a new global player in vaccine production and distribution to be subject to WHO pharmaceutical standards and approvals.

Africa is watching in shock this rise of health as an instrument for geopolitics and geo-economics. For instance, Russia's prospective Coronavirus vaccine is named Sputnik V, a name that conjures up the Cold War. It was Sputnik I that became the first to successfully orbit into space, triggering the Space Race with the US in 1957.

Further afield, in Tokyo, the four nations of the Quadrilateral Security Dialogue, the US, Japan, Australia and India, held a meeting of foreign ministers recently. Among the things discussed was the development of a Covid-19 vaccine aimed at countering China's. Those developments are quite disturbing for the most vulnerable nations affected by the virus. They pose a potential threat to poorer nations as they could be forced to endorse diplomatic initiatives against their national interests.

There is no doubt that at this juncture the priority is finding a vaccine for Covid-19. The long-held people-centred solidarity in tackling global pandemics is being replaced by inward solutions such as Trump's 'America First'. The heightened tension between the US and China is undermining cooperation among scholars and students across the world. There have been endless cases of Chinese students in American universities perceived as being spies of the Chinese government.

The US is the main anchor in global vaccine research and production, but Trump's attempts to interfere in the Covid-19 vaccines have the potential to undermine US leadership in this global arena.

It is hoped that Africa will make good use of all the help it can get as a response to the Coronavirus. The temperament of significant partners, such as the current US administration, demonstrates just how erratic the international system is. The continent will have to relook at the depth of its interactions with other parts of the world and how less emphasis on intra-African synergy could expose the continent to the fickle nature of international politics.

There's a lot riding on the outcome of the US presidential election in terms of Africa's relations with China

A Trump victory in the 3 November US elections is likely to see the US intensify its attempts to roll back China's successful Africa policy. A Biden administration will find areas in which its US-Africa policy will converge with that of China. The US and China will be more likely to cooperate within multilateral forums and will actively seek a multilateral approach to global challenges such as peacekeeping and health matters.

The United States democracy is too big and fortified to completely collapse. However, the controversy over Russia's alleged involvement in the 2016 elections and the events of the last four years have shown that indeed America's democracy is not completely impregnable. The 3 November 2020 US elections are rightly perceived as 'generational elections'. More than anything else, those elections will become a major landmark and point of reference in the history of the United States. They stand to make or break not just President Donald J. Trump but America itself, as a global hegemon.

On Wednesday, 21 October 2020, the African Centre for the Study of the United States, based at Wits University, will hold a timely virtual town hall meeting open to the public. African and American scholars will debate the vexing questions: What does the US election outcome mean for Africa-China, Africa-Europe and global politics? Why should Africans be concerned about the state of American body politics and, more so, its elections? Where do China and Europe fit – in both the outcome of the US elections and their implications on its own quest for development?

First, Africa invested heavily in human capital (African-Americans constitute 13.4% of the total 328,239,523 US population, according to the July 2019 estimates of the US Census Bureau), raw material and knowledge in the development of the US's economy and its electoral politics.

As a country that depicted itself as a 'City upon a Hill', the US is no stranger to Africa's politics. Its footprints are seen in all phases of the continent's political and economic life. It has also influenced Africa through its soft power by expanding education through missionary schools. Many nongovernmental organisations from the US have also been instrumental in advocacy work across Africa. Most of the founding leaders of African national liberation movements and current leaders in different fields were educated in the United States; the US therefore played a critical role in shaping what we consider as African politics.

More importantly, the US intervenes in Africa's electoral politics and often plays a critical role in its development through investments in infrastructure, health, education and trade, with the African Growth and Opportunity Act (Agoa) being the main trade agreement. In doing so, it competes with other players such as the EU and the rising China. The outcome of the upcoming elections carries heavy implications on the African continent. Due to those factors and more, it is in Africa's interest to pay great attention to the new direction of the US policy towards Africa and the world after 3 November 2020.

I intend to dispel outright three major assumptions erroneously made by observers of the US elections. First, the elections are about American domestic politics and the illiberal Donald J. Trump – a leader who has undoubtedly sledgehammered the liberal international order largely built by the US in the post-World War 2 system. The second assumption that those observers make is that the US democratic system is 'remarkably stable and self-regulating'. Third, Trump's ruinous four years have accelerated the decline of America's economic and global leadership and, should Joe Biden win the election, his administration will likely reverse all of the above.

There are structural changes taking place in America's real and indeed perceived global power. The US-China rivalry will continue, and Africa is going to be a stage where it openly plays out. The US will intensify its attempts to roll back China's successful Africa policy.

Graham Allison and Joseph Nye have both rung the alarm bells about America's standing in the global arena. A 25 October article by Allison in *The National Interest* declared: 'China Is Now the World's Largest Economy. We Shouldn't Be Shocked.' According to Allison, we should not be shocked because China has already displaced the US as the largest economy in the world.

Washington insider scholar Joseph Nye has laid out five US future scenarios: 1) the end of the globalised liberal order; 2) a 1930s-like authoritarian challenge; 3) a China-dominated world order; 4) a green international agenda, and 5) 'more of the same'.

Regardless of who wins the November election, Trump or Biden, the United States will not be the same. There is little to say about Trump's 'America First' foreign policy and its destructive impact on US relations with allies and foes. Although it is increasingly becoming unlikely that he will win, if he does, some of the bleak futures that Nye imagined will certainly come to fruition.

The greatest danger in that scenario is the high likelihood of heightened tensions that could result in accidental wars in the South China Sea that aggravate the India-China border dispute and the dispute between China and Taiwan as well as on the African continent, where US and Chinese troops face each other in Djibouti. Advanced weaponry, nuclear and otherwise, needs leaders who have a level-headed temperament. The twenty-first century belongs to Asia, and Africa's trade with that region is high. Any disturbances in Asia will impact the continent adversely.

There are structural changes taking place in the US's real and indeed perceived global power. The US-China rivalry will continue, and Africa is going to be a stage where it openly plays out. The US will intensify its attempts to roll back China's successful Africa policy.

The first area in which the US will lock horns with China in Africa will be that of infrastructure building. Washington will exert its weight within international financial institutions such as the Bretton Woods to restrict poor African countries from signing new infrastructure deals with China. That will come under the so-called 'debt trap' narrative. Although the debt trap narrative comes as a genuine altruistic move to protect poor Africans from what it perceives as an expansionist China, the main motives are none other than stopping China's Belt and Road Initiative, an alternative route to the current US-dominated routes in global trade.

Agathe Demarais, the global forecasting director at The Economist Intelligence Unit argues in the *South China Morning Post* that even if Biden wins, 'there's little perspective for meaningful improvement in US-China relations … The two countries will remain locked in a strategic competition for economic and technological dominance.'

However, China has an upper hand in Africa because, while America talks negatively about China, it does not have an alternative solution. In other words, talk is cheap: for example, American hi-tech companies do not have an appetite to invest heavily in Africa's hi-tech industry.

There are, however, high chances that a Biden administration will find areas in which its US-Africa policy will converge with that of China. The US and China will be more likely to cooperate within multilateral forums. First, Washington will certainly rejoin the Paris Agreement on climate change and also return to the Joint Comprehensive Plan of Action nuclear deal with Iran. In addition, Washington will actively seek a multilateral approach to global challenges such as peacekeeping and health matters. Such a move will see joint Washington and Beijing efforts boosting Africa's Agenda 2063.

Still at an international level, a Biden victory might revitalise the US's participation in the Trans-Pacific Partnership. We might see a US that is once again committed to being a rational leader, not inward-looking as has been the case under the Trump presidency. Once again, there is a lot riding on the impending election, as it has the potential to change not only the US but the globe in fundamental ways.

Daily Maverick / Opinionista / 15 December 2020

Huawei wars: Joe Biden's ascent to US presidency a ray of hope for multilateralism

Unlike the US-USSR Cold War rivalry, the Sino-American rivalry is between two giants whose economies are inextricably intertwined. Thus, in crude terms, China poses a greater threat to the United States than did the Soviet Union. Nowhere is that more heated than in the technological sphere.

The election of Joe Biden as the next president of the United States, at the expense of Donald Trump's bid for a second term, is undoubtedly a ray of hope for multilateralists. The Trump administration was a divisive edifice with no clear policy direction, save for satisfying Trump's atavistic desires for untrammelled power, domination and fealty. He won the surprise 2016 election by appealing to the baser instincts of human nature, deflecting responsibility for one's problem onto a perceived threat.

In terms of the US's economic and employment challenges, Trump blamed it on his predecessor's alleged incompetence and China's unfair trade benefits. He vowed to get American jobs back from China and that he would punish China for what he said was their gaming of the international system.

As president, Trump felt compelled to carry through some of his campaign promises. No political realist could blame him for that because his rhetoric granted an unexpected victory and thus, it was understandable that he would not depart from what he thought was a winning formula. Knowing very well that he was woefully unsuited to be president, Trump never ceased to campaign, and his rallies were invariably laced with the hate-filled oratory of his pre-presidency campaigns. As one who wanted to 'make America great again', Trump had a special place for China in his armoury of anti-globalist positions.

The United States has, for the last three quarters of the century, been accustomed to being at the summit of the international system. Its peerless economy and its dominant role in military and technological spheres gave the

United States unprecedented influence on global affairs. During the Cold War, the Soviet Union posed the only, if distant, competition to US dominance. Today, however, the US faces China's steep competition in almost all fields.

Unlike the US-USSR rivalry, the Sino-US rivalry is a rivalry between two giants whose economies are inextricably intertwined. Thus, in crude terms, China poses a greater threat to the United States than did the Soviet Union. One area in which the jostle for dominance in the ensuing world system will be more heated is in the technological sphere.

One of the biggest heralds of China's technological ascent is telecoms equipment-maker Huawei Technologies Co. Ltd, founded in 1987. Huawei is now the world's biggest producer of telecoms equipment. The company states that it 'guarantees that its commitment to cybersecurity will never be outweighed by the consideration of commercial interests'.

Despite Huawei's assurances of cyber safety and independence from the Chinese Communist Party, which is essentially the Chinese government, the company is constantly forced to respond to endless allegations levelled against it by its competitors and China's detractors. It is often accused, without any shred of evidence, of working in tandem with the Chinese government to spy on people at the behest of the CCP.

In May 2019, the United States added Huawei and 70 of its non-American affiliates to the Entity List. The Entity List is a compilation of businesses, research institutions, governments and individuals that enjoins those listed to get a special licence in order to export, re-import or transfer products subject to Export Administration Regulations.

That also 'meant that suppliers who normally supply Huawei with US products (including software updates and other technology) would no longer be able to do so without a licence from the US'. In other words, Huawei and all entities that appear on the List are perceived as threats to US security. Huawei was added to it on the assumption that it is engaged in activities that are inimical to US national security.

The US's allies, chief among them the United Kingdom and Australia, are persuaded by US fear. Britain's Huawei Cyber Security Evaluation Centre (HCSEC) deals with areas of concern pertaining to Huawei's approach to software development. In September 2020, HCSEC issued its 2020 annual report, the sixth of its kind, which is based on January 2019 to December 2019 annual activities. The report noted that while 'HCSEC satisfied its requirements regarding the provision of software engineering and cybersecurity assurance artefacts to ... the UK operators as part of the strategy to manage risks to UK national security from Huawei's involvement in the UK's critical networks', it still reserves concerns about Huawei's software developments – concerns that might jeopardise the UK's security.

The report accused Huawei of not upholding its guidelines on matters such as coding. Those misgivings dovetail with those of the National Cyber Security Centre, a UK body that offers support to private and public consumers of cyber products 'to make the UK the safest place to live and work online'.

Australia, in the same manner as the UK and US, also went on to ban high-risk vendors from its 5G roll-out, with Huawei and ZTE particularly singled out. Predictably, China has taken umbrage at such measures, characterising them as bias and discrimination. At a political level, the conduct of the UK and Australia in espousing US positions conjures up memories of how the UK erroneously and disastrously followed the US into the war against Iraq.

Notwithstanding possible dangers that might come with any form of technology, the assumption of the US is that it could convert any power to its mode of looking at world politics, with the bandwagoneers doing so unthinkingly. Africa is one of the regions where the United States will pontificate about the dangers of Huawei-sponsored technology. African giants such as South Africa have already made great strides in using Huawei. Africa has to exercise a great deal of sovereignty and vigilance as it consumes technologies that emanate from beyond its shores. The risks, however, should not and must not be levelled against one company, Huawei alone, as most biased analysts do.

It appears that Huawei will never satisfy its detractors, as the more it answers security questions, the more new questions are posed. According to Gabriel Wadi, 'Securing digital networks requires a coordinated international response – an outcome that the Trump administration's actions have yet to produce.'

Intergovernmental collaboration is required: countries need to work together and talk to each other because cybersecurity is not only about data flow within domestic boundaries but between countries in terms of service trade, e-commerce, culture exchange and international cooperation on law enforcement.

Furthermore, within its personnel, Huawei commits about 46 per cent of those to research and development, asserts that security is in its DNA and that 'security requirements are embedded into how we design, build and deliver all our products'.

Finally, in Africa's case, and indeed in the case of any players who might be under duress to jettison Huawei technologies, they have to assert their sovereignty and respond to that pressure with the certainty that digital surveillance, where it exists, is not an exclusively Chinese phenomenon.

Politics behind China's stance on Hong Kong

The protests in Hong Kong, now in their fourth month, must be an encouraging index of sovereign ambitions to China's detractors and competitors. On the surface, the protests are a laudable crusade for democracy and an attempt to insulate Hong Kong from China's governance.

It is also important to note that the 'One Country, Two Systems' pledge, to which China committed itself after Hong Kong was handed over to it by the UK in 1997, forms part of the rationale for what the protesters argue is China's encroachment on Hong Kong's semi-autonomy. Over the years, successive leaderships in Hong Kong have styled themselves as trustworthy.

It is no wonder, then, that those who support the protests in Hong Kong have a Manichean interpretation of the continuing demonstrations: it is a fight by the honourable (protesters) against the dishonourable (the Chinese government and their lackeys in Hong Kong). At the heart of the matter lies politics, which, by nature, like any social terrain, is a consequence of historical factors whose destination is never certain. Political structures are steeped in history. People, as agents, shape history. The political future is also something that, even though it could be planned, has the potential to mutate as unforeseen eventualities could impose the necessity for tinkering with original plans.

Therefore, China's position on what is happening in Hong Kong should be looked at from a historical standpoint. The island of Hong Kong was ceded to the British Crown in 1842, as inscribed in the Treaty of Nanking. That forfeiture was a culmination of a humiliating period in China's political history at the hands of a foreign invader. China's woes at foreign domination did not end with the loss of Hong Kong.

In the twentieth century, Japan carried out one of the most wanton destructions of human life ever experienced by Asia on Chinese soil. The invasion of Manchuria added a violent notch to China's already inflamed siege mentality.

It is no wonder, then, that China played such a pivotal role in helping Third World countries snap the shackles of colonial and minority bondage. It did so to the extent that it almost appeared suicidal and masochistic: for example, to help end Zambia's dependency on minority-ruled Rhodesia (later named Zimbabwe after independence) and apartheid South Africa, China put up a generous loan of more than US$400 million towards building the Tanzania-Zambia Railway.

That commitment was made in the late 1960s when China's per capita GDP was lower than that of sub-Saharan Africa. Those realities create a background to what is happening in Hong Kong and why China feels that the rest of the world should not shape the course that Hong Kong should take.

It would be beneficial for the youth, especially, to understand the historical factors that underpin China's reluctance to adopt foreign-bred modes of rule and its antipathy to foreign encroachment, whether ideological or physical. In *The China Wave: Rise of a Civilizational State*, Zhang Weiwei, an erstwhile interpreter of Deng Xiaoping, highlights the *sui generis* (unique) nature of China as a state.

In his arguments, while China will open up to the rest of the world, it will not lose its distinct identity as a civilisational state. It is therefore understandable that since it will exercise fidelity to the 'One Country, Two Systems' template, no one is under illusions about China's preference to not only harmonise Hong Kong and Beijing but to bring Taiwan into the fold as well.

What China will seek from the rest of the world is understanding and respect, rather than censure and criticism. As it has shown obeisance to non-interference in the internal affairs of other nations, it will expect repayment of that favour as it seeks to resolve the conflict that has engulfed Hong Kong.

G7 held in climate of uncertainty and misunderstanding

Last weekend, G7 countries met in Biarritz, France, to discuss pressing global issues such as climate change and Iran's nuclear ambitions. Historically, the G7 is an exclusive group of the world's most industrialised economies.

The unifying characteristic of the G7 was support for the post-1945 world order underpinned by liberal internationalism, multilateralism and globalisation. Russia was suspended from the group in 2014 after a brief membership, having joined in 1998, due to the crisis in the Crimean Peninsula.

With each Summit, the G7 is fast losing its bearings, vision and direction. The 2019 Summit was held under a climate of misunderstanding and uncertainty. Less than a week before the Summit, Giuseppe Conte, Italy's prime minister, expressed his intention to resign from the government.

Since the last G7 Summit in Canada, the United Kingdom has changed its prime minister. It is noteworthy that none of the two changes in leadership has come at the end of a regular term of office. The changes spoke of the uncertainty that is gradually taking hold among G7 members.

Donald Trump has added to weakening consensus among the G7. His insistence that Russia be readmitted to the group has not received a lot of support from fellow G7 countries. Indeed, readmitting Russia will challenge the identity that the G7 seeks to present. If it champions liberal democracy, then it cannot condone Russia's seizure of Crimea.

Apart from the Russian dynamic, Trump compounded G7 problems by imposing steel and aluminium tariffs on members of the G7. That said, the main questions to be asked are: Does the G7 retain the lustre that it once enjoyed as a group of stellar economic and industrial economies? Second, what lessons, if any, does the G7 offer to the rest of the world?

In answering the first question, the G7 no longer represents the world's elite economies. From the G7's founding in the 1970s, the economic landscape of the world has changed tremendously. Japan has been outstripped by China as the world's second-biggest economy.

Boris Johnson is also expected to assume a similar position to Trump. Angela Merkel, who has often been the voice of reason and a calming presence in the G7, will resign in 2021, which could be a loss of a redeeming feature of the G7 unless there has been a positive change of leadership in other member countries.

There are palpable fears that Matteo Salvini might become Italy's prime minister, which would add yet another member to the G7 whose views on immigration are controversial at best.

That possibility brings into sharp focus what Merkel's retirement might mean. What does the weakening fabric of the G7 mean for Africa? President Emmanuel Macron scored some political points by inviting non-G7 members to France during the Summit. It is laudable that a good number came from Africa, and South Africa was among them.

Unfortunately, Africa has no say on how the G7 should be configured and where it should focus. What is clear is that with insular politics becoming more prominent in the West, Africa can scarcely be sanguine about the future of the G7.

That should offer more incentive for Africa to look for partners who could help the continent surmount the many challenges it is facing. The US and the UK, under their current leadership, do not offer much appeal.

Now could be the time for fortifying the ideals of Agenda 2063 and the African Continental Free Trade Agreement and augmenting intra-African trade. Africa could thus form a formidable group of the continent's countries, forging a path that will guarantee development.

As a caveat, however, that priority should not close off the rest of the world, as the US and UK, whether by design or default, seek to do.

Golden era of summit seasons for Africa

Leaders of 54 African countries and international organisations will gather once more in Yokohama, Japan, next week from 28–30 August, for the 7th Tokyo International Conference on African Development (Ticad 7).

Since the inaugural Ticad 1 in 1993, the World Bank Group, the UN, the UN Development Programme and the AU Commission have been partners in that summit.

For Prime Minister Shinzo Abe, Ticad 7, under the theme 'Advancing Africa's Development through People, Technology and Innovation', provides him with a golden opportunity to achieve several strategic foreign policy goals for Japan.

First, haunted by the country's unsettled aggressive WW2 record in the region, especially in South Korea and China, Japan seeks to strengthen its relationship with the African continent.

Second, Japan also wishes to regain ground in the infrastructure development space, a field it widely perceives to be losing to its arch-rival, China, in Africa. Abe will certainly use Ticad 7 to rebrand Japan in Africa in line with his muscular foreign policy.

Due to the large numbers of African countries' membership in the UN system (they constitute a third of the UN membership), the continent is an important one for any country seeking a positive global influence. In 2018, more African leaders attended the Focac Summit in Beijing than the UN General Assembly in New York. While the US-Africa Business Summit was held in Maputo, Mozambique, almost two months ago, President Vladimir Putin will have his Russia-Africa show with African leaders at Sochi in early October. So this is a golden era of summit seasons for Africa.

Japan has already agreed with India to counter the Chinese-led Belt and Road Initiative through their India, Japan and Asia-Africa Growth Corridor.

African leaders must avoid getting entangled in Japan's ideological jabs against China's Africa policy. Japan uses Africa to fight China.

It is widely reported by Japanese newspapers, such as *Japan Today*, that Tokyo plans to include 'concern' over excessive debt, or the so-called Debt Diplomacy, in the declaration of the Ticad 7, which is in line with Washington's language to discredit Beijing in Africa.

According to Japanese Foreign Minister Taro Kono, 'international assistance should be provided in accordance with international standards such as transparency, openness and economic efficiency.'

Those principles are crucial components of Japan's quality infrastructure initiative.

African leaders should avoid the usage of ideological phrases as well as the winner takes all mentality akin to the Cold War era that Japan uses in distinguishing itself from China.

Confronted by a fast-shrinking working age, Japan is looking at employing some of the African students studying at its universities upon their graduation. Africa should welcome Japanese assistance in training its people; however, that should not cause a brain drain on the continent.

Unfortunately, strict Japanese adherence to the Organisation for Economic Co-operation and Development and unwary support for the US's Africa policy stands to undermine its Africa policy. To win in Africa, Japan ought to abandon its previous Cold War mentality. Throughout the Cold War, Japan supported Washington's policy in Africa.

In South Africa, for example, the Japanese government unashamedly accepted 'honorary white' status to fit into the apartheid system.

Boris Johnson talks big, but can he deliver Brexit?

Number 10 Downing Street's new occupant, Boris Johnson, has undoubtedly shocked the world as the Conservative Party's chosen leader. Britain, therefore, joins the US, Philippines, Ukraine and Brazil with famous leaders whose cantankerous personalities defy logic. South Africa has fresh memories of such leadership.

One does not have to go any further than Parktown in Jo'burg, where the drama of former President Jacob Zuma's years in power continues to be displayed at the Zondo Commission.

Johnson is not Donald Trump, Rodrigo Duterte, Volodymyr Zelensky, Jair Bolsonaro or our own Zuma. BoJo, as Johson is famously known, has had an equally colourful character and career as a journalist, mayor and foreign secretary.

Johnson's leadership has, however, brought about a new era in global politics in which governance is no longer based on good character and a proven record. The new British PM's history is littered with lies and awkward views. His accession proves that anyone can be a leader these days, as long as you can tap into people's worst fears about open borders, immigration and cultural dilution.

Will Johnson succeed in uniting a divided Britain? As the chief advocate of Brexit, can he negotiate a better deal with the EU than his predecessor, Theresa May? What can Africa expect from number 10 Downing Street with Johnson as the resident?

Johnson inherits a profoundly fragmented and divided Great Britain in search of its place in Europe and the world. The main challenge confronting all British PMs since Winston Churchill has been a declining economy compared with other countries in Europe and the world.

Since 1945, Britain has been recovering from a shrinking empire with its colonies gaining independence.

Britain has witnessed a gradual decline in global leadership since US hegemony began asserting itself over the world. Unfortunately, Johnson belongs to those revisionist Britons longing for the lost imperialist past. The Brexit that Johnson championed is primarily predicated on wishful thinking and a desire to bring back Britain's glorious past.

Johnson will undoubtedly prioritise the relic of the Commonwealth, which once more defies logic as some of the former British colonies such as India, Canada, Australia, New Zealand and South Africa occupy relatively high positions in global politics. For instance, India's economy surpasses Britain's.

It won't be long before Johnson tests the power of the EU on the matter of Brexit. All of the enthusiasm he showed on his victory day last week will end in Brussels when he faces the EU leadership over the issue.

He is unlikely to get a better deal than May, and it will soon be apparent that he is neither sufficiently competent nor capable of bringing fresh ideas and plans to steer Britain out of domestic challenges and the EU. Instead, Britain under Johnson will lose the influence it currently commands within multilateral institutions.

Attempts to resuscitate the Commonwealth will fail dismally, as many countries are looking to China and other bodies, such as Brics, for leadership on matters of global governance.

What about Africa? Former British PM Tony Blair's disastrous Zimbabwe policy and the perception of Africa as a 'scar on world's conscience' will not be rescued by Johnson. He thinks that 'the Commonwealth is to be thanked for providing rows and rows of flag-waving piccaninnies'. He will also figure out that the so-called piccaninnies are moving forward with the AfCFTA to negotiate new trade deals with Britain as equals.

The world is also eagerly waiting to see if Britain will continue its pretence of being a significant power and colonial master of unfolding events in Hong Kong.

Migrant problem is not just African

In Niamey, Niger, this week, African leaders took the extraordinary decision of officially launching the African Continental Free Trade Area (AfCFTA), a critical pillar of Agenda 2063, a step towards the ideal of pan-Africanism.

Shockingly, however, the AU didn't pay sufficient attention to the war crimes committed against African migrants in Libya.

Last Tuesday, the Tajoura Detention Center, outside Tripoli, which housed roughly 610 people, mainly Africans, was bombed, leaving more than 50 migrants dead and at least 130 wounded.

All credible reports point to Khalifa Hafta's Libyan National Army to have committed that dreadful act. The irony is that the current chairperson of the AU, President Abdel Fattah el-Sisi of Egypt, supports Khalifa Hafta and his murderous bandits.

Hafta has numerous backers, and chief among them are the usual suspects, the US and France – countries that headed up the destruction of Libya and the assassination of its leader, Muammar Gaddafi, in 2011.

The UN High Commissioner for Refugees (UNHCR) estimates that there are at least 10 million stateless people globally.

Sub-Saharan Africa had a total of 721,326 stateless people in 2014. According to the Institute of Statelessness and Inclusion (2014), the UNHCR identifies South Africa as one of the six countries in Africa (including the Democratic Republic of the Congo, Eritrea, Ethiopia, Madagascar and Zimbabwe) where there are significant challenges, but there is no supporting data.

That situation has been worsened by endless wars of choice fought in Iraq, Libya, Syria and Yemen. Africa confronts constant factors that force people out of their countries. The bulk of migrants, including those stateless people, remain within the African continent.

However, a small number of refugees take treacherous journeys through the Sahara Desert to Libya, eventually trying their luck to access Europe through the Mediterranean Sea.

Several thousand migrants have perished on those modern-day self-enslavement voyages to Europe, fleeing from bad governance, conflict, unemployment, hunger and worsening climate change. Most of them remain Eritreans, Somalians, Ethiopians, Sudanese and others from Nigeria, The Gambia and Senegal.

As much as the migrant issue remains an African problem, the US and Europe are equally to blame. How can we explain the allegations of the involvement of some of our closest allies, such as Russian mercenaries, in the slaughtering of African migrants while we stand and look?

The only African response from Addis Ababa is the usual well-crafted standard statement, 'We condemn.' What about the reactions of Africa's other leading countries such as South Africa, Nigeria, Kenya and Ethiopia? There has been a deafening silence from those capitals in the aftermath of those atrocities. Those leading countries in Africa must strongly call for action to be taken against Khalifa Hafta.

Khalifa Hafta is a naturalised US citizen. He was a former confidant general of Gaddafi, with whom he staged the 1969 coup that ended King Idris's reign and ushered in Gaddafi's rule of four decades.

However, Hafta was captured in Libya's war with Chad in the mid-1980s. As a result, he settled in Virginia in the US, where he stayed for 20 years.

When President Obama, working closely with France, attacked Libya in 2011, Hafta was fronted as a trusted general who could stabilise the country.

When one pays attention to President Donald Trump's attitude towards migrants, it becomes clear that, under current circumstances, if one were searching for a moral lodestar and luminary of championing the cause of the world's most vulnerable populations, the US is the last place of recourse.

The Mercury: Opinion / 26 June 2019

China-Africa trade expo a unique opportunity for Africa

Tomorrow and Friday, China will host the first China-Africa Economic and Trade Expo in Hunan Province. In addition to the more than 50 African countries that have confirmed their participation, several international bodies such as the UN Industrial Development Organisation, the World Food Programme and the World Trade Organisation will send representatives.

At least 1,000 Africans are expected to attend the Expo as guests or traders. The event is a further demonstration of the ever-growing Sino-African relationship, which traverses a gamut of issues, from historical similarities, political affinity and an economic reliance to the recently deepening people-to-people relations.

Last year, China-Africa trade reached US$204.2 billion (R2.9 trillion), up 20%, year-on-year. China has been Africa's largest trading partner for 10 years; thus, the Expo seems to be an expected initiative between two parties who have had an impressively growing relationship.

African entrepreneurs, alongside their Chinese counterparts, will showcase their products, no doubt culminating in bilateral trade and infrastructure agreements. The Expo will coincide with the G20 Summit in Osaka, Japan.

With the Sino-US trade tensions offering a cheerless backdrop to what portends to be an awkward Summit, issues concerning the developing world are not expected to dominate the debate. The Expo thus assumes even more importance in an international system that is currently undergoing a resurgence of ultranationalism, insular sentiment and antipathy towards immigrants who are not of Western provenance.

While that context is regrettable in an era where globalisation is expected to imbue the world with tolerance and acceptance of significant cities, primarily as cultural and national melting pots, it provides the developing world with an opportune impetus to concentrate on being principals and arbiters of their regions and affairs.

For almost the whole of Africa, China has become an indispensable player in helping the continent to surmount its myriad challenges. While Sino-African trade and economic ties have grown impressively, Africa remains rooted to the foot of the global food chain.

The opposite is the case with China, a country that, just four decades ago, was an agro-based, underdeveloped, poor economy but has risen to become the second-biggest economy in the world. By next year, China plans to eliminate poverty among its citizens.

Lin Songtian, China's ambassador to South Africa, often evokes the estimated 700 million people that the Chinese government has lifted out of poverty since the advent of economic reforms in 1978.

Prevailing circumstances have seen a surge in private Chinese and African citizens trading places between the regions to put down roots in their respective countries. While that is in kilter with the trend of globalisation, it has also precipitated tension that emerges from ignorance of each other, as well as racial confrontation and the scramble for economic opportunities.

Opportunities such as those offered at the Expo should be used to demonstrate China's good intentions as it relates to Africa. It's encouraging that since the onset of the US-China trade war, Africa's non-traditional exports such as meat, fruit, nuts and tobacco have improved. Trademap estimates that meat exports to China from the Southern African Development Community have improved by 240%.

If that momentum is sustained, it will help Africa to invest more in land, climate change and hydro technology. The Expo will have a lasting legacy if it touches on that.

Pretoria News: Opinion / 19 June 2019

Forging a new developmental path for Africa

There was no better place in which to reflect deeply on the role of African elites both in government and the private sector than Addis Ababa. I could not stop thinking about the aspirations of African leaders as they met in that great city in 1963, establishing the Organisation of African Unity, now the AU.

The failure of African liberation movements across the continent was mainly caused by their inability to think independently outside the logic of colonialism. They inherited colonial structures that imposed strong constraints on liberation politics, which resulted in the perpetuation of colonial-era configurations.

The fundamental goal of the African struggle was national liberation, which was defined as political independence in a sovereign state under a government representing the majority of the previously colonised people, who had been excluded from full participation in society through the colonial and apartheid systems.

Pan-Africanism, the enduring vision of African liberation, identified the struggle for social and political equality and freedom from economic exploitation and racial discrimination as a common underlying theme. However, it did not clearly articulate the content, ideology and character of the postcolonial state.

The elites, who assumed control, postcolonialism, embarked on state capture, in which they treated their countries like personal fiefdoms and used the resource spoils of power to entrench and retain their authority.

The celebration of independence/transition to democracy was premature in the context of its discontents: the elites viewed the state as a front of authority and privilege, while the majority of African citizens continued to wallow in poverty.

The apartheid state was the epitome of social and economic injustice. It was characterised by a systematic legal and institutional framework to ensure white domination through preferential treatment for whites while depriving

Blacks of assets they needed to support their livelihoods. It is in that context that one watches, with great interest, the arrival of a new generation of leaders in most African parliaments.

As President Cyril Ramaphosa delivers the State of the Nation Address this week, a significant number of parliamentarians from the #FeesMustFall movement will be present. That generation of youthful leaders must inject fresh ideas into Parliament.

The starting point would be to reimagine government policies as people-centred. There is an urgent need to ensure that Parliament plays its constitutional role in holding the executive accountable. What makes other nations succeed compared with the African continent is the prioritisation of meritocracy over royalty on matters of governance.

Most leaders in crucial, strategic positions in government have been recycled, although they failed dismally to change the status quo. Do not expect recycled leaders and policies to produce desired results. It is vital to consider a developmental state that does not tolerate corruption.

Particular attention should be taken to revive, not dismantle, state-owned enterprises in the advancement of appropriate infrastructure for the majority of the people on the margins of the economy. There are inherent limitations in the ability of the current colonial- and apartheid-inspired states to deliver economic freedom to African people. Therefore, think beyond the confines of those fragmented African states. Think and act regionally and continentally.

Trade wars will overshadow economic talks

President Cyril Ramaphosa will join fellow G20 leaders at the G20 Summit to be held on 28 and 29 June in Osaka, Japan. The Summit will be held against an inauspicious backdrop with the two major global economies locked in a trade war. The Sino-American trade war has global consequences and stems from deeper issues than those cited by the two belligerents.

Utterances coming from Washington betray paranoia and a reluctance to admit that China is inexorably challenging a unipolar world order without changing its political identity. Writing in *Foreign Affairs* (January/February 2019), Professor Yan Xuetong predicts that 'rather than vie for global supremacy through opposing alliances, Beijing and Washington will largely carry out their competition in the economic and technological realms'.

The ongoing trade war and the three-nation Huawei saga perfectly typify Xuetong's thesis.

Speaking at the International Institute for Strategic Studies (IISS) Shangri-La Dialogue Defence Summit, Singaporean Prime Minister Lee Hsien Loong said, 'The bottom line is that the US and China need to work together, and with other countries too, to bring the global system up to date and to not upend the system.'

Beyond Sino-US wrangling, the EU will also attend the Summit, shortly after European elections in which right-wing, populist and anti-immigration political groups made gains, confirming that, even though rhetoric to exit the EU might somewhat subside, anti-immigration is in vogue and is winning support across Europe.

For Africa and other emerging powers, the Summit could be of great benefit – if it will bring to fruition the aspirations expressed by Japanese Prime Minister Shinzo Abe. According to him, 'Japan is determined to lead global economic growth by promoting free trade and innovation, achieving economic growth and the reduction of disparities and contributing to the development agenda and other global issues, with the Sustainable

Development Goals at its core.'

Through those efforts, Japan seeks to realise and promote a free and open, inclusive and sustainable 'human-centred future society'.

Like Donald Trump, Jair Bolsonaro, Brazilian President since January this year, has threatened to withdraw from the Paris Agreement, stating that the environmental policies are suffocating and could preclude economic growth and industrialisation. For a country that was once a beacon of ecological friendliness, Brazil under Bolsonaro is increasingly becoming a threat.

The coming G20 Summit will undeniably take place in an uncertain climate, and it will be interesting to note what form the leaders' agreement will take, should they agree on one.

As Africa's only member of the G20, South Africa carries a considerable responsibility going into the Summit, and it will ill forget that, in 2020, it will assume the presidency of the AU.

Even though Ramaphosa was only recently elected president, he will still be expected to play a leading role in championing the cause of emerging economies at the Summit. South Africa itself faces internal economic challenges, with its growth expected to be 1%, at most, for 2019.

Those cheerless realities form a background against which South Africa will attend the G20. With the largest number of developing economies, Africa hopes that Abe's expectations for the emerging economies will come to pass.

Unfortunately, the Sino-US trade war, the Sino-Canadian diplomatic row and the likely divergence over climate change among G20 member states are likely to overshadow the urgent need to take into serious cognisance the plight of emerging economies.

What the trade war between China and the US means for SA

What a remarkable inauguration on a perfect African day: after the ANC's victory in the national elections on 8 May, Cyril Ramaphosa was inaugurated as president on 25 May.

The message was never lost: South Africa is back on the world stage after nine ambivalent years.

The *Thuma mina* (Send me) message goes beyond South Africa's shores, vibrating across the continent that Pretoria will actively serve the interests of the continent.

That daunting task, however, won't be stress-free. When Ramaphosa's predecessor, Jacob Zuma, entered the Union Buildings in 2009, the global financial crisis had just begun. Now, President Ramaphosa faces what is clearly becoming the 'Digital Iron Curtain', triggered by US restrictions placed on Chinese tech companies such as Huawei.

When Ramaphosa joins fellow G20 leaders from 28–29 June in Osaka, Japan, trade war tensions will continue to overshadow other matters affecting the world, especially Africa. Since the 2016 G20 Summit in China, African issues have been receiving significant attention.

South Africa and the AU have collectively worked tirelessly to connect the AU's 2063 Vision with the UN Sustainable Development Strategy for 2030.

Ramaphosa's most formidable challenge at this year's G20 Summit will be how to raise Africa's challenges of poor infrastructure, high unemployment and slow integration to global partners.

Japan seeks to 'achieve a human-centred future society that will be free, open, comprehensive and sustainable'. There is no doubt that the Japanese agenda draws from Confucianism, a philosophy found across Asia that shares similarities with Africa's values and norms of ubuntu.

Unfortunately, the norms and values advanced by Japan stand in the way of 'America First' notions propagated by President Donald Trump. The trade conflict between China and the US could be understood from the background of insular politics in the US to China's advocacy for a future of shared humanity.

Under such circumstances, what does the Sino-US trade war have to do with South Africa?

The forthcoming G20 meeting will no doubt be held among countries that have assumed antithetical outlooks on the global political economy. South Africa will be tasked with a delicate balancing act. First, it should not surrender its sovereign perspective on the current pulse of international politics. Second, there seems to be no easy way of galvanising a unified G20 in a way that could benefit South Africa and Africa in general.

Thus, one alternative would be to exact commitments from individual members of the G20 such as China and Japan. Unfortunately, the Trump Administration has not enjoyed general support in Africa; hence, the US might increasingly forfeit its allure as a global leader. Its reluctance to accept emerging realities about China's prominence might also force China into a militant position.

It is hoped that the polarised nature of global politics will not impose on Africa a Manichaean dilemma of a 'you are with us or you are not' nature.

It is almost certain that Democrats, who should typically take a different, more inclusive and liberal stand on international affairs, will be lured into the fear-mongering that Trump is whipping up.

With the seeming popularity of nationalistic sentiment taking hold in much of the West, no ambitious politician would want to style him/herself as being soft on a competitor as formidable as China.

Amid all of those cheerless possibilities, it is hoped that Africa will not be sidetracked from pursuing its objectives. South Africa should play a leading role in that respect.

Africa would do well to steer clear of tussle between US and China

Dr Kiron Skinner, US State Department Director of Policy Planning, elicited opprobrium for characterising China's 'threat' as the first time the US 'will have a great power competitor that is not Caucasian'. She also said the jockeying with China is 'a fight with a really different civilisation and a different ideology'.

Such talk during the US-China trade war, between the biggest and second-biggest global economies, respectively, could only stoke the conflict.

Adding race to America's paranoia over China is reminiscent of the 'Yellow peril' anxiety, which perceived people of the East to be existential threats to the West. South Africans who endured the apartheid system will remember how the *swart gevaar* (Black danger) calcified racial chauvinism.

At the 2019 Conference on Dialogue of Asian Civilisations, China's President Xi Jinping asserted, 'The thought that one's race and civilisation are superior and the inclination to remould or replace other civilisations are just stupid. To act them out will only bring catastrophic consequences.'

The expressions of both Skinner and Xi Jinping evoke Samuel Huntington's Clash of Civilisations theory. He argued that in the post-Cold War era, conflict would be characterised by a clash of civilisations in the form of a plethora of identity cleavages, ranging from cultural to religious.

Islamic fundamentalism, the resurgence of ultra-nationalism and Western hostility towards China's rise seem to justify Huntington's forecast. The main point of contention between the US and China resides in how they view their place in the world.

Former US Secretary of State Henry Kissinger, a panjandrum of realpolitik, wrote in his book, *On China* (Penguin, 2011), that US exceptionalism is missionary, sees its values as universally applicable and is inclined to convert the rest of the world to the US world-view. At the same time, China's exceptionalism is cultural and seeks only that other countries understand and tolerate its world-view.

Thus, China does not impose its values on others. The ongoing trade war is redolent of Cold War politics. Of particular interest to Africa is how the continent should react.

During the Cold War, Africa was only useful as a tool for winning ideological battles and fighting proxy wars on behalf of the US and USSR. Rebels, dictatorships and looters, such as Jonas Savimbi in Angola and Mobutu Sese Seko in Zaire (the DRC), received Western support because they were deemed a buffer against the spread of communism. The instability and ruin they wrought in their countries were subservient to expediency.

Now, Africa seems to have an instinctual leaning towards China's world-view because, with its history of being colonised, Africa is naturally hostile to foreign imposition, and China does not impose its world-view on Africa. Its seeming respect for other countries' internal affairs is an effective soft power tool that draws former colonies to China. But Africa's posture in the international system should not be a reckless decision elected to distance the continent from the West and former colonial powers.

From the early 1990s, the collapse of the Soviet Union betokened victory for market economics and neoliberal democracy. Africa responded favourably. To date, the continent has embraced Western political values and economics, however improperly. On a continent where people have tasted the right of electing their governments, it would be a severe drawback to be seen to adopt a system that curtails people's choice of who should govern.

Consequently, Africa should assume an autonomous position from both China and the US. It is thus heartening to note that South Africa has refused to be drawn into the Huawei saga, with the Department of Trade and Industry stating that South Africa does 'not discriminate against any international companies but treats foreign companies like local companies'.

African agency entails that it seeks to improve its circumstances by being the principal decision-maker of where the continent should head. Both China and the US have redeeming features that could improve Africa's lot. China has shown that, with foresight, the right ideas and the political will to implement them, Third World countries could surmount difficulties. But the US view of democracy and respect for human rights seems to have taken root on the continent. Ultimately, Africa will have to chart its way, but it should never again suffer the indignity of being an exploitable footnote in the tussle among big powers.

US: out of step and out of line?

The art of dancing requires the ability to listen prudently to the rhythm of music to align one's body's moves to its beat. Increasingly, the US's responses to a rising China resemble a dancer without rhythm.

As a dancer, Washington has demonstrated that it is both a clumsy ballerina and a poor listener of the fast-paced rhythm of post-Cold War music. That is particularly true when one watches the US dance to the songs played from Beijing.

In the post-World War 2 era, the US mastered the Containment dance. When the Soviet Union threatened Western capitalism through the spread of communism, Washington devised a well-coordinated dance in response to the music emanating from Moscow.

Although the dance was clumsy at first with the rise of McCarthyism, Washington perfected the Containment dance abroad by deploying different moves for different regions.

Once again, the US has reinvented a dance for the new era and object of containment: China.

Like the Soviet Union, China seemingly poses a grave danger to American hegemony. Surprisingly so: China does not seek to spread any ideology in the world.

Although Beijing adheres to communism with Chinese characteristics, it practises a variant form of capitalism, mainly led by the state. Thus, it poses no threat to Washington's market economy.

Despite that reality, Washington deploys similar strategies and tactics in response to the meteoric rise of China as it did during the Cold War.

The first clumsiness in Washington's responses to China predates Donald Trump's administration. When Brics countries established the New Development Bank, the West generally reacted negatively, perceiving the South-South cooperation as a threat to the World Bank and the IMF. It responded similarly to the Asia Infrastructure Investment Bank.

The developing world, especially Africa, needs more development funding than what existing development finance institutions can afford.

Second, the US has responded poorly to the BRI led by China. In 2018, bipartisan legislation was enacted with the sole purpose of countering the BRI in Africa through the 'Better Utilisation of Investments Leading to Development Act' or Build Act. As a result of that act, Washington will open the doors of the International Development Finance Corporation (IDFC) at the end of this year.

With only a US$60 billion (R850 billion) budget, according to Washington, the IDFC's main aim is to 'create more robust and flexible investment tools for US companies to create employment and help support small and medium businesses in Africa'.

That budget is insufficient to achieve strategic objectives. It is an amount equivalent to what Beijing commits to Africa annually. It is also the amount China committed to Pakistan alone. The entire BRI has a total budget of US$1 trillion.

Instead of diverting some of an enormous sum of money from the defence budget to development, the US, known as the force of destruction through its endless wars in Afghanistan, Iraq, Libya and Syria, would prefer to apportion its finances to more controversial causes.

Third, Washington's response to Huawei's superior 5G technologies exposes its weaknesses rather than showing global leadership in science and technology.

In all of the above, Washington demonstrates a lack of innovation to compete with China. It is increasingly difficult for Washington to convince its allies in Europe to abandon Chinese-led BRI or use of Huawei technologies.

Against that backdrop, Africa could be well counselled to avoid being used as a tool for ideological competition among the mightier powers in the international system.

IOL News: Opinion / 17 April 2019

Russia must avoid booby traps set by West in Africa

With Robert Mueller's investigations into alleged Russian meddling in the 2016 US elections halted without finding a 'smoking gun', the anti-Putin brigade have turned to Africa in search of Russia's footprints.

That comes at a time when Moscow signalled its desire to renew its relationship with Africa. African leaders and heads of state will be in Sochi, Russia, from 22–24 October for the Russia-Africa Summit to strengthen that relationship.

But what appears missing in the African-Russian foreign policy calculus that flourished in the Cold War Era is how to avoid booby traps. Those are not only made in the US but also the post-Cold War African political environment. The challenge for Russia's Africa Policy comes from Washington and its European allies eager to limit Moscow's political and economic influence in Europe and the world.

President Vladimir Putin's prolonged stay in power, the annexation of Crimea in 2014, the backing of the Bashar al-Assad regime in the Syrian civil war and, more importantly, being the most reliable and cheap source of gas in Europe, stands in the way of US hegemony.

Moscow is also frustrated at the US and its allies' actions in Zimbabwe, Venezuela and Myanmar within the United Nations Security Council by using its veto power. 'Russia advances its political and economic relationships with little regard to [sic] the rule of law or accountable and transparent governance,' said President Donald Trump's National Security Adviser, John Bolton, when he launched the US-Africa Policy.

When African and Russian leaders meet in Sochi, Jacob Zuma, Jose Eduardo dos Santos, Robert Mugabe, Abdelaziz Bouteflika and Omar al-Bashir will be absent. Those staunch friends of Russia – 'Russia's Africa' – have fallen like dominoes. Moscow ought to learn from its perceived corrupt relationship with certain African leaders, e.g. in the failed nuclear deal with South Africa.

It is crucial that Moscow resets its foreign policy towards Africa informed by a new set of norms, values and mindset.

Russia has an advantage in Africa due to its solidarity with the struggle against colonialism and apartheid during the Cold War. But that era has come to an end. Africa has entered a new phase of work to liberate its people wallowing in poverty, disease and other calamities such as climate change.

Russia does not need to compete with the US or China in Africa. It must find its diplomatic and economic niche.

Russia should avoid propping up corrupt leaders who use violence to maintain power in Africa. It should invest heavily in the African youth, particularly in science and technology, where Russia excels. Russia and Africa could build a win-win relationship if Russia enters into agreements with African countries in the beneficiation of raw materials, development of the ocean economy, health and space. In all of those fields, Russia has a comparative advantage in its renewed Africa Policy.

Russia appears to have lost ground in Africa in the post-Cold War era, but its prospects to succeed in Sochi and Africa are predicated upon Moscow's ability to devise a smart and innovative foreign policy.

Russia ought to realise that competition in Africa does not only come from the US and China. Many other players seek opportunities in Africa. The aftermath of the collapse of the Soviet Union's empire drastically diminished Moscow's influence in Africa. President Putin rightly perceived that 'as the major geopolitical disaster of the century'.

What Russia should avoid in its Africa Policy are perhaps the pitfalls of being driven by the desire to go back to the glorious empire of the Soviet Union during the Cold War era. If Moscow avoids the booby traps set by its foes in the West and pushes for accountable leadership and good governance, that can be achieved.

A global Britain? That is UK's task now

Theresa May's Brexit pickle is all about how to deliver a Brexit while maintaining British standing in the international arena and her leadership. It is increasingly clear that May will be the last prime minister at Number 10 Downing Street to enjoy the country's long-held trappings of soft power.

Simply put, the dilemma May faces will be how to fortify Britain while advancing the slogan of 'Global Britain'. Britain's weakening economic fortune and high levels of disunity demonstrated throughout the Brexit period do not provide sufficient grounds to sustain the Global Britain agenda. That is because Britain has neither sufficient financial resources to underwrite Global Britain nor the national unity to drive such a plan.

From its time as an empire builder, the United Kingdom has always had global influence and, in some quarters, allure. The formation of the Commonwealth was one way the UK used to maintain ties and sway with the territories it once ruled as colonies.

The success of the Commonwealth and UK's soft power resided in the fact that countries that were not erstwhile British colonies, such as Mozambique and Rwanda, successfully lobbied to be included in the Commonwealth. Even countries that had left the Commonwealth, such as The Gambia (which has since returned) and Zimbabwe, formally submitted intentions to return.

Since joining the EU in 1973, the UK has been a significant player in the organisation, bolstered by its permanent membership at the UN Security Council.

The economic synergy that was formed by the EU, coupled with the obliteration of visa requirements among EU members, made the EU a model of regional integration after World War 2 and the Cold War.

Those factors also lend credence to the UK's intent to be a political example to those to whom it preached democracy and human rights. It also presented itself as a power that was poised to march in tandem with the increasingly globalising world that attracted international travel.

The referendum presents the UK as a power that wants to retreat from regional and global integration, indeed as a power that is succumbing to the nationalistic sentiment that is sweeping the West after the rise of terrorism.

The UK will have a difficult time convincing its allies, even in the Commonwealth, that Brexit does not translate into withdrawing from global responsibility.

The election of Donald Trump in the US might reinforce the attitude that the West is gradually forfeiting its soft power and shirking its global responsibilities.

That is in stark contrast to erstwhile minor powers who are spreading their appeal through economic and political ties. China is chief among those who have commendably ensconced themselves in Africa. At the time when Britain is leaving the EU, China is in the incipient stage of leading the Belt and Road Initiative. That project will cater to more than 60% of the global population: the initiative befits the trends of globalisation.

The concept of Global Britain, however, seems a last-ditch effort to hang on to the influence that the UK is gradually ceding. Thus, even though the Commonwealth is likely to retain its current membership, it is unclear how much importance its members will attach to it.

Africa needs to fully understand Brexit to enable it to respond to a changing Britain. There will be more room to negotiate new Free Trade Agreements with the UK after Brexit.

Diplomats dropped the ball with leaked memorandum

Glued to their televisions watching the dramatic Zondo Commission and its revelations of former president Jacob Zuma's nine years that were lost to corruption, South Africans woke up to a sideshow.

The usual suspects, the US, UK, Germany, the Netherlands and Switzerland, claim to be champions of democracy, human rights and anti-corruption. But those countries' diplomats dropped all diplomatic niceties. They leaked a memorandum they collectively wrote to the media demanding that President Cyril Ramaphosa deal decisively with corruption and stop 'South Africa's frequent changes to policies for industries, including mining and the protection of intellectual property rights'.

They failed to respect the well-established tradition in international relations of communicating with the head of state through the country's diplomatic missions abroad and the foreign affairs ministry.

Surprisingly, those meddlers decided to leak their ill-conceived and executed memorandum at a time of high global tension due to the events in Venezuela. Those very same meddlers in South Africa's electoral process are also actively interfering in that Latin American country.

Unlike in South Africa's case, in Venezuela, the muddlers unashamedly endorsed the unelected opposition leader, Juan Guaido, who claimed himself as the interim leader on 23 January this year.

What can we read into the memorandum to President Ramaphosa? Could it be a veiled threat to Pretoria's steadfast opposition to the coup in Venezuela?

That memo came while South Africa was preparing for general elections. The US, UK, Germany, the Netherlands and Switzerland could not wait for the State of the Nation address to hear President Ramaphosa's short, medium- and long-term positions on the clean-up exercise in the country's institutions of governance.

It would have made more sense to hear President Ramaphosa address the nation on sensitive matters such as anti-corruption measures, policy prescriptions for his administration, including mining, property rights and Black Economic Empowerment before issuing a memorandum.

Shockingly, the US, UK, Germany, the Netherlands and Switzerland embarked upon their action at a time when they are themselves blaming Russia and China for interfering in their electoral processes.

It is imperative to note that corruption in South Africa has an international dimension. There are global companies in South Africa, including those from the five countries named above, who are actively participating in corrupt activities.

Rather than teaching others about the norms and values of democracy, the diplomats from the US, UK, Germany, the Netherlands and Switzerland should spend more time building democracy at home. They should also assist South Africa in resolving the legacy of colonialism and apartheid through land distribution and the involvement of its Black majority in the mining sector.

More importantly, those diplomats should not be hypocritical. They should not blame Russia and China for interfering in their electoral processes while they are engaged in acts of sabotage in Venezuela.

South Africans overcame one of the most brutal systems in the world – apartheid – so there is no doubt that they will overcome the erosion of democracy under Jacob Zuma's presidency. That can happen if our diplomats know their place. They can also help our country in its attempts to fight corruption by monitoring their companies involved in tax evasion and corruption.

Africa the odd one out at G20 Summit

Overwhelmingly outnumbered is the African sentiment about the upcoming Summit in Buenos Aires. South Africa, as usual, is the solitary African voice at the G20 Summit where the world's more 'industrialised' (read Western) powers will discuss global matters.

In line with tradition, criticised since the 1884 Berlin Conference, the major economies meet to discuss economic growth, the sustainable use of natural resources, climate change and promoting equal opportunities and inclusiveness.

The Berlin Conference was viewed, owing mostly to Basil Davidson's documentary, *The Magnificent African Cake*, as a crime against humanity because it reduced an entire continent's people into unwilling participants in European industrialisation and development.

The blatant exclusion of African states in decisions affecting the global economy and other world issues is palpable. Each continent seems to have relatively adequate representation, with at least two G20 member states, North America and Europe, having the lion's share.

The one-sided global directive coming out of those engagements is deliberate because a significant addition of an AU to feign balance would provide support for the lowly South African voice. However, it would disturb the stage-hogging giants.

Weeks after the G20 curtain-raiser summit for finance ministers and Monetary Fund governors of the G20 nations, the now official communications channel from the White House (the daily tweet from the master bedroom lavatory), sent out a message about recent positive talks regarding trade with China. That message was echoed by President Xi Jinping on CGTN regarding his openness to meet the US and foster a mutually beneficial partnership in the G20's corridors.

Those pre-emptive engagements are to be concluded in Argentina in a climate of diplomacy. The global markets reacted almost immediately after a risk-averse period with the rumblings of a trade war where the US subjected Chinese products to tariffs to the tune of US$250 billion (R3.5 trillion). China responded with tariffs of its own worth US$110 billion. The Asian and US markets showed gains, indicating that conflict and protectionism are not only anti-development but also bad for business.

The US-China trade relations will surely eclipse the more politically correct items on the Buenos Aires Summit agenda – global profits and revenue maximisation tend to do more to inform international policy than people's needs.

That is especially concerning for the sole African participant at the Summit because the rhetoric of improving people's lives rings no truer than in Africa. This continent is the most desperate for development and inclusive growth enjoyed by the rest of the world but sadly is the most ostracised. The G20's structure and mandate prove that.

A contingency plan at the 2017 Hamburg Summit was the G20 Compact with Africa during the G20's German presidency. It is the proverbial bridge with the G20 and African nations, as it is open to all African countries to increase sustained private-sector investment. That German-initiated forum met last week for a review of progress made.

But it seems to have become a bilateral affair, with most of the outcome featuring Ramaphosa and Merkel strengthening their ties through a Bi-national Commission and increased cooperation in the UN Security Council amid large investment pledges made by German companies during the Investment Conference in South Africa, a week earlier. It honestly seems that profits garner more attention than people.

So in Argentina, Ramaphosa will have to balance national interest and the African agenda. It is critically important for South Africa to focus on investment and aligning itself with the big players. Africa's concerns need to be seriously discussed on the G20 agenda.

Ethiopia's rise out of famine and war has world's attention

During my teenage years in the early 1980s, I remember that Africa's worst case of war, famine, disease and poverty was in Ethiopia.

For Americans, it was a golden era when the US marshalled soft power at the height of the Cold War. Although the liberation movements in southern Africa were politically aligned to the former USSR, we could not resist as children the US's soft power channelled through music, movies and Western media, including the likes of CNN.

I remember watching traumatising news about the famine in Ethiopia. The country under Mengistu Haile Mariam fought a devastating war with Siad Barre of Somalia, as the USSR was imploding, bringing to an end the Cold War.

Ethiopia and Somalia had followed different paths. Somalia disintegrated and became a failed state when Siad Barre's regime fell during a civil war. In Ethiopia, an insurgent Ethiopian People's Revolutionary Democratic Front led by Meles Zenawi defeated the dictator Mengistu Haile Marian ushering in a developmental state. Ethiopia drastically changed from a country defined by famine, war, disease and poverty to one that sheds a bright light on the African continent.

Former president Thabo Mbeki hailed Zenawi, saying in September 2012 that he was 'a great architect of the new Ethiopia'. Geographically well located on the Horn of Africa, Ethiopia is the continent's second-most populous nation (with 102 million people in 2016), after Nigeria. It is close to the Middle East and serves as the gateway to the world's second- and third-largest economies, China and Japan.

There is nothing that will stop Ethiopia achieving its dream of reaching a lower-middle-income status by 2025, as its economy has registered an impressive growth rate of 10.3% since 2005. Ethiopian Airlines remains Africa's most profitable airline, reaching more global destinations than South African Airways and Kenyan Airlines. Ethiopian Airlines is in the early phases of building yet another airport in the Bishoftu area, 48 km from Addis Ababa, with a projected annual capacity of 80 million people.

If Zenawi was the 'great architect of the new Ethiopia', the current Ethiopian leader, Abiy Ahmed, appears to be a peacemaker with a developmental plan for the wider region. He has wasted no time in ending the senseless war with neighbouring Eritrea. The peace with Eritrea is part of Ahmed's broad strategy of reforms in Ethiopia. He has filled half of the national parliament with female MPs, breaking with the tradition of having a male-dominated national assembly, like most African countries.

In recent weeks, the prime minister has appointed female scholar and diplomat Sahle-Work Zewde to the position of president. Although that remains a largely ceremonial position, it has nonetheless sent a positive signal to Africa's male-dominated body politic.

Ahmed has vowed to continue with his predecessors' economic agenda, the second phase of its Growth and Transformation Plan: the Grand Ethiopian Renaissance Dam is halfway complete.

The Dam is expected to supply Ethiopia and its neighbours with much-needed energy to power economic development in the region. The new Chinese-built 750 km Ethiopia-Djibouti railway has shortened the time it takes to get goods to and from port. Ethiopia is attracting more investment from China and is becoming an alternative destination for Chinese companies. The country has already earmarked itself to be Africa's manufacturing hub. The world's attention remains fixed on South Africa and Nigeria as the most vibrant African economies. Still, it seems that Ethiopia will soon have a seat at the table with the giants.

It won't be long before more people from South Africa and Nigeria head to Ethiopia for a better life. Ethiopia's poverty curse has been lifted.

Mutual benefits for unequal partners

Chinese and African leaders will mark the 15th anniversary (2000–2015) of the Forum on China-Africa Cooperation (Focac) this week in Johannesburg under a fast-changing global order with enormous implications for all parties.

The Peoples' Republic of China has tremendously transformed as a country since the Bandung Conference held in Indonesia in 1955. According to Brian Bunting, the ANC was represented by Moses Kotane and Maulvi Cachalia, who observed the proceedings of the Conference. An under-developed China, plus Asian and African countries (with the bulk of them still under the yoke of colonialism and apartheid), called for economic cooperation, cultural cooperation, self-determination and the promotion of world peace.

It was critical that China sought solidarity with countries from the Global South for its economic development and survival in a global order defined by the Cold War. At the time, China was in its sixth year since the establishment of the PRC on 1 October 1949.

The current prestigious position that Beijing occupies as a permanent member of the United Nations Security Council (UNSC) was only possible due to the overwhelming support it received from the Global South, mainly African countries in the United Nations General Assembly in 1971. In demonstrating its appreciation for the political backing received from Africa, China supports the position of the continent within the institutions of global governance, such as the UNSC.

In the current world order, the Chinese position has fundamentally transformed. China has become the world's second-biggest economy, while Africa's position remains mostly peripheral.

As in the early decades of its establishment, China still needs Africa. It is pursuing a multi-pronged strategy to garner a larger share of global power befitting its global ambitions. Africa, however, is still battling for its fair share of that global power through representation in the international institutions of political and economic arenas such as the UNSC, the World Bank and the IMF.

However, China is undergoing a sharp economic slowdown. It is also confronted by the rising tensions in the South and East China Seas, triggered by territorial disputes with Japan, the Philippines, Vietnam and others in the region. The pivot by the US to the area, perceived in Beijing as a move to constrain China's peaceful rise, has exacerbated the situation to a high point of potential conflict.

In response to those obstacles, Beijing has pioneered two significant initiatives: the Asia Infrastructure Investment Bank (AIIB) and the New Development Bank (NDB) or Brics Bank. Those have helped China roll out the famous One Belt, One Road and the twenty-first century Maritime Silk Road, spreading its economic activities far and wide in the regions of the world, including East Africa's city of Mombasa.

China needs a large share of Africa's infrastructure projects for most of its state-owned enterprises, which are steadily expanding their reach, globally.

Although China appears to be rewriting the rules of the game (written and dominated by Western countries) by leading in the establishment of the AIIB and the NDB, it still needs to play a larger role within the transformed IMF and World Bank. As the Focac takes place in Johannesburg, the city is joining other global cities as a leading hub for the Chinese currency yuan or renminbi. The IMF has recommended that China's renminbi be part of the IMF's Special Drawing Rights as the fifth currency.

In all of the above, China requires Africa's rising middle class as a market for its finished goods. In recent years, Chinese universities have gained more ground in the world rankings and have attracted more African students. Although Africa's rise is irreversible, its economies continue to haemorrhage due to the global economic crisis, the decline of the worldwide commodity boom, the impact of the Ebola epidemic, mainly in West Africa, and the periodic destabilisation caused by terrorist organisations such as ISIS in Libya, Boko Haram in West Africa and Al-Shabaab in East Africa.

The African Union's Agenda 2063 forms the basis on which Africa negotiates with China and other strategic partners. African Union Chairperson Nkosazana Dlamini-Zuma envisions a continent with 'high-speed railways, a common language, diplomatic clout, cutting-edge fashion and leadership in space exploration: that is the vision of a transformed Africa'.

The call made by President Xi Jinping in his September speech at the United Nations General Assembly for global cooperation and partnership marks a significant shift in China's role within multilateral structures. That speech signalled a positive move demonstrating a willingness by Beijing to increase its support for the countries in the Global South, particularly to achieve the newly adopted set of Sustainable Development Goals.

China has also become the largest contributor of peacekeepers among the five permanent members in the UNSC. It also played a significant role in combating the Ebola epidemic in West Africa.

African leaders should and must present a common position during the Focac. The relationship between China and Africa has matured enough to allow frank assessments of gains and losses by Africans in their engagements with their Chinese counterparts. While China enjoys Africa's support within multilateral structures, it ought to support the AU's call for the transformation of the UNSC, the IMF and the World Bank.

Through Focac, African leaders and their Chinese counterparts can take their relations to new highs through frank discussions.

What is undeniable is the fact that both China and Africa need a peaceful global order to achieve their respective developmental goals and dreams. Therefore, negotiating for a peaceful world, as was the case at Bandung in 1955, should drive Focac. China must use its economic muscle, while Africa must use its resources and voice to transform the global order.

Interlude

I spent a great deal of my formative years in Mozambique and Zimbabwe. Like any typical youth in the bread basket of Africa around the 1980s, I was obsessed with music and more specifically British Pop music. So you can imagine my emotional state when I caught a glimpse of Bob Geldof's *Live Aid* concert in 1985. It was like I was part of the sea of 72,000 people packed to the rafters at Wembley Stadium in London that day.

I sang along to every song from Phil Collins and Sting, to Freddy Mercury's Queen and George Michael and Elton John. I was smitten, and even tried to sing along to the single compiled by a large group of performing artists called 'Do They Know It's Christmas?' – but even then, in my adolescent heart and mind, I detected something dubious about that picture. A stage full of white people singing to hordes of other white people under the pretence that they are concerned that the starving children in Africa may not be aware that it is Christmas. What kind of hellish universe must be so cruel so as to withhold Christmas from children. But I was a child in Africa, and I knew about Christmas and was nowhere near starving. I neither had flies on my face nor had ever been recruited into a child army. However, I understood that in some places, that was the reality but wondered how knowing about Christmas would help them and whether they would even care.

I was confused. Why did such a prolific musical spectacle have to exist under a banner of African poverty and desolation? The subtle racist undertones were unmistakable. It was a popular theme at the time. The Americans on the other side of the Atlantic pond like Michael Jackson, Lionel Richie, and Stevie Wonder did 'We Are the World' and called themselves USA for Africa. I knew a vastly different Africa, and it seemed that someone was giving people overseas a drastically different view of us and our home than the view we have of ourselves. It seems that the problem was the source and slant of international news and general information about Africa and Africans. Ours is a vast and abundant continent with equally different and fascinating people – some waring, aggressive and generally hostile and others passive to the level of flaccidness, even in the face of crisis. We are not, as imagined by 400 years of colonialist misinformation, one thing, but are an array of peoples living in vastly different lands and in dramatically different ways.

Publications and networks such as CNN in the 80s and 90s seemed to revel in the idea of starving African children with flies on their faces and bulging kwashiorkor stomachs. It is no wonder that Americans and Europeans commoditised that eerie image and filled stadia to party and feed the 'starving children of Africa' simultaneously. But that was a far cry from the reality of millions of Africans. Africa was and still is a place of rich heritage and pride-filled people who carry an almost innate sense of community and humanity. As with any place on Earth, there are conflicts and challenges. Some of them are true atrocities and crimes against humanity, not unlike other territories, globally, that have experienced similar events.

What is unique, however, with Africa's conflicts is that they occur as a result of indirect rule implemented by former colonialist powers. When African states regained independence, the bureaucratic structures of governance employed by colonial powers persisted and eventually caused conflict among the various indigenous peoples and cultures. The disconnect between the messaging on mainstream media and what I knew to be the reality for Africans was what drew me to the study of Global Politics and International Relations.

There was no mention of the Berlin Conference of 1884, where European powers divided the African continent among themselves and proceeded to pillage resources to their colonial empires. They set up stopover ports along the African coastline to service their voyages on trade routes to India and the rest of Asia. Come African independence, the systems of governance that established ruling classes based on cultural and linguistic lines were invoked to create favourable relationships with former colonial powers to continue natural resources extraction under the claim of bilateral partnerships.

The European markets had developed a demand for African raw materials and with more and more traffic in ports from trade, the coastal port cities became strategic areas of power for whomever controlled them. The internal conflicts from the inequality between indigenous groups resulted in many post-independence civil wars across the continent. Many of them, under the strain of failed government institutions, experienced a lack of food security and famine. That is why we must tell our own stories.

One such conflict was the result of the Belgian occupation of Rwanda. The Belgians' preference for the minority Tutsis, who they deployed into administrative roles in government, exacerbated the pre-existing divisions among members of different cultures and ethnic groups. That was further intensified by the Belgian film-maker Harmand Dennis and his depictions of various ethnic groups in Rwanda. In 1994, the perceptions of different groups came to a tipping point with the radio station, Radio Television Libre des Mille Collines blaming the Tutsis for the downing of the president's plane and calling for their annihilation. In less than 12 months, 800,000 people had perished. The international community and mainstream media failed to raise the alarm by declining that that was a genocide until it was too late and the horror had reached peak insanity.

As academics and scholars of post-conflict areas, I was invited to Kigali with a team of other such people to document the genocide. One day, we travelled about half an hour outside the city to a church. When we approached, we could see scraps of clothing and debris, and when we got there, the stench of hatred and rotten corpses disturbed the air. It was unlike anything I'd ever seen. I would have been disturbed and moved to strong emotion if it weren't for my mind's desperate plead for me to wake from that nightmarish scene. I prayed and begged for those poor souls. Hollow-eyed and cracked bony temples on the table, on the floor and in every nook and crevice for as far as my eyes could reluctantly see. I was charged to be there, teary-eyed and all. My eyes had to stay wide open and not give in to looking away: they had to take it all in, if only just to respect the silenced ones that filled that room. To plead for them and witness their tragic and horrific demise so that no one else would have to experience it.

In the aftermath of those conflicts, African countries need to rebuild. After years of unrest, they borrow to finance their infrastructure development objectives but get into debt with the IMF and World Bank. The Structural Adjustment Programmes they had to agree to as a prerequisite trap them into that vicious cycle of debt. They use their natural resources to secure their loans and, in a bit of twisted logic, they sign up for a type of neocolonial deal that keeps raw materials and gross production from African states in the hands of Europeans through their financial institutions.

Africa's attempts to source financing partnerships for their infrastructure development endeavours from anyone other than Western powers have been labelled as neocolonialism by former colonisers. It is high time African problems are viewed through an African lens and resolved by Africans ourselves. Maybe we could save ourselves a world of trouble and pain that seems to haunt us as remnants of our colonial past and legacies.

African Politics

Pretoria News: Opinion / 22 January 2020

AU must take ownership of African matters

Once again, Karl Marx's instructive statement that history repeats itself, 'first as tragedy, then as farce', is at play in Europe.

The first Berlin Conference of 1884–1885 united imperialist powers in sharing the spoils of colonialism by breaking up Africa into the current 54 fragmented countries.

The usual suspects, joined by the resurgent Russians and Turks, met once more in Berlin to hold a summit that sought to find a peaceful solution to the raging conflict in Libya.

African representation and voice at the imperialistic gatherings has been mute, other than Egyptian President Abdel Fattah el-Sisi, who will hand over the AU chair to President Cyril Ramaphosa at the 33rd AU Summit in Addis Ababa from 9–10 February this year.

El-Sisi, who will leave behind a dubious record as the AU chair, presents a Janus face, thus advancing peace and security through an inclusive negotiation while backing one of the rebel groups in the Libyan conflict.

The Libya file will be the hottest among the many Ramaphosa will get from his predecessor. Libya could be either a redeeming or poisoned chalice for Pretoria. It is thus pleasing to see Ramaphosa abandoning the UK-Africa Investment Summit to prioritise the mammoth task of preparing the handover of the chair to South Africa.

There are many reasons why South Africa's move is smart. First, Ramaphosa being paraded among African leaders in London and shaking hands with UK Prime Minister Boris Johnson would have looked bad.

Second, although the UK remains a strategic partner for South Africa and Africa, it is not China. The UK's economic and diplomatic power after Johnson's Brexit is on the decline.

Third, South Africa was complicit in the bombardment of Libya by supporting the France-UK-US-sponsored UN Security Council Resolution 1973, which used 'all means necessary' to destroy Libya. South Africa as AU chair and a champion of the African Agenda 2063 cannot be seen mingling with forces that pretend to be Africa's friends while aiding the destruction of the continent.

Ramaphosa will be reinforcing the AU's theme for 2020 – 'Silencing the Guns'. In Libya, Russia and Turkey are reported to have mercenaries on the ground. When the US was under Barack Obama's leadership, the UK and EU bombed Libya under the pretense of spreading democracy. The real reason was to control its oil.

Ironically, neither Russia nor Turkey played a part in the 2011 conflict that toppled Libyan leader Muammar al-Gaddafi. But it appears that their interests are converging with those of the UK, the US and France, the initial countries who brought us to the current situation, who pretend to be peacemakers and mediators but support General Haftar. The AU has been rendered toothless by foreign powers jockeying for control of Libyan oil.

In 2011, the AU wanted the crisis to be resolved peacefully through negotiation and power sharing, and they pleaded with Western countries to give peaceful resolution a chance.

Perhaps Ramaphosa ought to revive an African approach to peace in Libya. A start would be to take ownership of the peace process under the AU's auspices. The Berlin Summit failed to bring any tangible agreement for foreign powers to stop interfering in the conflict by deploying mercenaries and dumping weapons. It also failed to uphold a UN arms embargo.

Haftar's Libyan National Army rebels, backed by Westerners and Russia, appear to have the upper hand. They have controlled some ports and oil pipes. The UN-backed Government of National Accord in Tripoli might not last long, as it is supported by weaker powers like Turkey, Italy and the AU.

Ramaphosa should reach out to all parties in Libya. The AU should reassert its authority over African matters and thus avoid summits that seek to undermine the African Agenda.

Henceforth, Ramaphosa should not attend Berlin, London and the earmarked Russian summit to discuss African matters. He should find a neutral venue in Africa and invite all parties to the conflict to negotiate a peaceful resolution – a move that could assist with silencing the guns in Africa.

Pretoria News: Opinion / 29 January 2020

Soft power needed at this crucial time

This year, when South Africa succeeds Egypt as the AU chair, its foreign policy behaviour will be affected, mainly by domestic circumstances.

South Africa has received a lot of goodwill from the world after emerging from almost half a century of apartheid and isolation. The Madiba magic that the Mandela presidency inspired lingers.

South Africa's exceptionalism on the continent has enjoyed what US political scientist Joseph Nye calls 'soft power'. That power, as opposed to coercive and physical power, bends other actors to one's will through attraction and appeal.

Through its practice of liberal democracy and market economics, coupled with an industrialised economy and reasonable infrastructure, it has been a choice destination for people fleeing war, conflict, economic desperation and inadequate infrastructure.

However, as Stephen Ellis warned in his book, *External Mission*, South Africa is losing its exceptionalism and becoming just another African country. There are many reasons for that caveat.

Corruption in South Africa, an age-old problem, seems to have become brazen, especially during Jacob Zuma's tenure as president, a period referred to as nine wasted years. Corruption gnaws at a country's soft power. The mismanagement of state-owned enterprises, a consequence of corruption and cadre deployment, has adversely affected the economy.

While President Cyril Ramaphosa is trying to correct the ills, his party is littered with individuals cited in corruption scandals that characterised the nine wasted years. He has attracted negative attention, emerging from how his presidential bid for the ANC was sponsored.

The domestic circumstances form challenges that diminish South Africa's standing in Africa and undermine the force and appeal of its foreign policy.

South Africa faces another Herculean task: its tenure coincides with the AU aspiration of silencing the guns by 2020. With its internal economic challenges, it will need help in terms of material and political wherewithal to meet the challenges Africa faces.

South Africa is taking over the AU chair from Egypt, a country that supports Libya's Khalifa Haftar, instead of the internationally recognised Government of National Accord. Ramaphosa will have to summon all of his diplomatic skills to deal with the impasse.

More physically immediate is the troubling advance of terrorism into Mozambique. As a more advanced power in southern Africa, South Africa will be expected to play a part in curbing the rising insurgency. South Africa also has to keep an eye on Lesotho, where a potential crisis is brewing. Lesotho, a country surrounded by South Africa, has its fate tied to that of this country. And South Africa's foreign policy will continue to be tested in the Democratic Republic of the Congo.

All of those daunting responsibilities will have to be accompanied by a two-pronged approach: South Africa will have to demonstrate domestic seriousness in reversing the mistakes of the past and, hence, reclaim its international appeal while taking up foreign policy positions that will be in tandem, especially with Africans. In the Libyan crisis, South Africa will have to be bold enough to denounce Haftar's machinations.

For South Africa not to be an isolated power, it will have to assume positions that will be attractive to the rest of Africa and demonstrate soft power. That again will demand difficult decisions.

Internally, the government will have to blunt voices from the ruling party that could sully the country's reputation. Ramaphosa will have to take advantage of the fact that, although many people are growing weary and wary of the ANC, there is reason in arguing that he enjoys more publicity than his party. Therefore, his foreign policy will have to reflect the realities.

Africa must shape its AI destiny

On 24 October 1956, Britain, France and Israel held a secret meeting in Paris to reverse President Gamal Nasser's nationalisation of the Suez Canal in Egypt – a global trading route and power symbol of the British empire.

When that ill-judged plan broke out in open war on 2 November of that year, President Dwight D. Eisenhower made it clear that the US would not support the move. Britain and its allies were forced to agree to a UN-led ceasefire, and that marked the ultimate end of British hegemony in global affairs.

Since the end of the Cold War, US multinational companies such as McDonald's, KFC, Amazon, Apple and Facebook spread across the globe. When McDonald's opened in Moscow's Pushkinskaya Square on 31 January 1990, it marked the beginning of US-led globalisation. That day, McDonald's served more than 30,000 hungry Muscovites eager to try tasty capitalistic diets. No one would have thought that in 30 years' time, US multinational companies would confront their most formidable competition from multinational companies in China.

Chinese telecom giant Huawei is a case in point. Since 1998, Huawei has grown exponentially, occupying the number-two spot after Samsung in the world. Spooked by Huawei dominance in Artificial Intelligence (AI), Washington placed strident restrictions on the company to avoid Chinese supremacy in the rolling out of the 5G-wireless infrastructure at home and abroad. That came at a time when Russian President Vladimir Putin predicted that whichever country led in Artificial Intelligence (including 5G) would dominate global affairs.

It therefore comes as a surprise that Washington's strongest and most-trusted ally, Britain, has effectively ruled in favour of Huawei playing an active role in the rolling out of non-security core 5G-wireless infrastructure. That is yet more British defiance of the US position on what it perceives as China's threatening rise. Britain also joined the Chinese-led Asian Infrastructure Investment Bank against Washington's wish to limit China's leadership in infrastructure financing.

Those moves have opened a wide crack within the US-dominated post-1945 World Order, and it appears that the debate will drastically shift from the US-led anti-Huawei narrative to broad discussions about global cyber-security.

African countries have joined Malaysia, Singapore, Indonesia, Brazil and others in doing business with Huawei. The US attempt to blacklist Huawei appears to be failing. It is important for South Africa and the rest of the continent to avoid targeting any specific multinational company. It is critical for South Africa, as chair of the AU, to lead in finding a multilateral solution in the governance of multinational companies involved in a sensitive field such as 5G-wireless infrastructure.

Africa should follow the excellent case made by German Chancellor Angela Merkel: that all companies involved in the 5G rollout should be seriously vetted to ensure that they comply with national laws. There are endless revelations from WikiLeaks and Edward Snowden that countries blaming Huawei for espionage have themselves been involved in eavesdropping on many world leaders.

Africa has refused to take part in the epicentre of the global power struggle for a cost-effective wireless infrastructure. The continent should be open for business to all international players in the rolling out of 5G. Given its large number of youth, Africa ought to embrace both Chinese and US companies without fear or favour. More importantly, Africa should actively participate in the creation of a rule-based environment governing the future of 5G-wireless infrastructure.

The spat between the US and China over Huawei is an opportunity for Africa to build technology. Africa remains a consumer of the high-end technological products of other countries in the West and East. It is vital for the AU and Regional Economic Communities to encourage member states to increase the funding of institutions of higher learning and learning hubs to innovate. Africa must play an active role in shaping the future of AI without being a victim of the power struggles for dominance.

Can the AU harness Africa's potential?

The AU appointed South African Wamkele Mene last week as Secretary-General of the African Continental Free Trade Area (AfCFTA), the world's largest trade area, to establish and run its trade secretariat in Ghana. Despite the wrangles between Pretoria and Lagos over that premier position, the establishment of the AfCFTA Secretariat signalled the crossing of the Rubicon.

Mene comes with vast experience and knowledge on trade and trade negotiation. However, to succeed, he requires an equally technical team and support from all member states, the business community and civil society. What are some of the major challenges the new secretariat will face? The rivalry between Pretoria and Lagos, the two biggest economies in Africa, might derail the mandate of a laudable initiative. As the economic giants of Africa, the two countries will have raised differences that, in the face of pan-African ideals, appear petty.

The AfCFTA comes at a time when multilateralism is losing its appeal. Those who once championed trade as a panacea to stunted growth now doubt whether that is the case. Increased economic inequality has also been cited as an indictment on the argument that trade improves growth. The withdrawal of the UK from the EU is one of the most glaring demonstrations of that anti-multilateral trend. African countries are thus moving against what is currently in vogue. Thus, getting the AfCFTA to work optimally will not be an easy thing to do. It is likely to be sullied by politics, as the prelude to Mene's election hinted.

Another caveat for the AU to bear in mind is that the trade area should not be a haphazard copycat of other institutions such as the EU. To bolster the movement of people and goods and to remove trade barriers, security will have to be increased across borders. Another warning is issued concerning the critical issue of funding and, *ipso facto*, influencing AfCFTA policies. For it to be an authentically African-owned initiative, its member countries will have to pool resources and cater for the attendant financial responsibilities that come with such a mammoth task.

Amid all of the formidable challenges Africa is facing, there is an upside to the continent. The implementation of the AfCFTA is a laudable milestone that will hopefully boost intra-African trade and realise the ideals of Africa's founding fathers and aspirations such as the Lagos Plan of Action (LPA) and Nepad. Intra-African trade still stands at less than 20%, but that could be easily changed through the smooth implementation of the continental trade agreement.

In 2019, some of the fastest-growing economies in the world were in Africa. While some major economies, such as South Africa, are projected to struggle, the African continent should harness the potential of smaller economies that have shown remarkable resilience. Ghana, where the AfCFTA's secretariat will be based, is one such economy.

By far the biggest asset that Africa has is its people. As the continent with the youngest population, Africa has more to win to secure a good future for its citizens. The more than a billion people found on the continent with a combined GDP of US$3 trillion (R45 trillion) could be a good platform on which to build a stronger continent. The basics of ensuring security and training for African citizens will have to be utilised for the better. The AU bears the responsibility for ensuring that.

The trade agreement should not only be based on trade because, as argued above, the merits of trade are being contested. More than anything, the ease of travel should ensure that skills are shared among Africans. Then there is the fact that African countries are at different stages of their industrial growth and economic and skills development. Those realities have been taken into consideration to ensure that the trade agreement does not bear lopsided benefits.

New trade era for Africa

As the dust settled from the three torturous years of negotiation with Britain over the terms of the Brexit severance, a large EU delegation jetted into Addis Ababa last week. It was led by the new European Commission President, Ursula von der Leyen, who eagerly wanted to hit the ground running.

The expectations of the EU Commission were simply to jet into Addis Ababa with its newly reconfigured EU-Africa Strategy and, keeping with the long-held hegemonic traditions, Africans would just ink the document without much serious negotiation and internal consultation.

To the disappointment of the EU Commission delegation and most pro-EU experts, the AU Commission Chairperson Moussa Faki did not sign the Strategy and instead raised numerous uncomfortable issues.

It is important, here, to highlight the timing and interesting aspects of that specific trip.

First, Africa has indeed emerged as a global actor after what Eduardo Soteras defined as 'overcoming a major hurdle to pan-African progress' with the signing and coming into effect of the African Continental Free Trade Area (AfCFTA) on 1 July this year.

Second, the Cotonou Agreement, signed in 2000 between the EU and the 79-country bloc of African, Caribbean, and Pacific states, expired on 29 February. The EU and Africa ought to speedily come up with a new trade agreement.

Third, Africa, unlike in the year 2000, has attracted myriad important new strategic partners ranging from the US, China, Japan, Russia, India, Brazil and the Gulf states.

Although the EU remains a critical partner for Africa, the continent requires more time to reconsider the new terms of trade agreements with all partners, especially the Cotonou Agreement. Obviously, with the AfCFTA in place and its secretariat being set up in Accra, Africa is no longer the same as it was during the era of the Organisation of African Unity (OAU).

The continent has to assert its newly found leverage as it renegotiates old trade agreements. Africa has 1.2 billion people and a mainly youthful market with an economy worth more than US$2.5 trillion.

The Cotonou Agreement should therefore be renegotiated with those factors in mind. The days of unfair trade, for instance in agriculture, wherein the EU continues protecting its farmers by subsidising them, are over. In the joint press conference between the AU's Commission Chairperson Faki and the European Commission's Von der Leyen, many other differences emerged.

The EU president specifically captured those differences when she said, 'Certainly, we have some differences: international criminal justice, sexual orientation and identity, the death penalty, centrality of the AU in certain crises – these differences are normal, given our cultural, sociological and even spiritual diversity.'

It was reported that some senior EU officials were offended by Faki's frankness in assessing glaring gaps in AU-EU relations. Those officials failed to understand why the AU Commission would raise differences with the EU without appreciating the EU's contribution to Africa's projects, which amounted to €274 million (R4.73 billion) last year. The notion of shared values between the AU and EU is flawed. The EU selectively nit-picks those values while maximising its interest.

Africa should relook its relations with the EU to ensure that they are balanced. More planning and consultation within Africa is required to ensure that the EU Strategy benefits both parties. Due to the incremental progress made on the continental integration shown by the signing of the African Continental Free Trade Area agreement, Africa ought to renegotiate all trade agreements with other partners. It is no longer business as usual. The lesson for Africa is that when it speaks with one voice, it achieves most of its political, economic and social goals.

China-Africa ties vital during Covid-19

Africa and China have shared a fascinating and resilient relationship. It is one that has been characterised by periods of solidarity and concerted effort to engender fairness in the international system. That background informs Afro-Chinese relations during these trying times beset by the Coronavirus.

Recently, Africa and China hosted the China-Africa Extraordinary Summit on Solidarity Against Covid-19. The Summit was led by China, Senegal (in its capacity as co-host of the Forum on China-Africa Cooperation [Focac]) and South Africa (as the current chair of the AU). Dr Tedros Adhanom Ghebreyesus, the director-general of the World Health Organization (WHO) also attended.

President Xi Jinping promised that China would help Africa with equipment needed to stem the spread of Covid-19. China also pledged to waive some of the debt due this year from African countries and to restructure time frames for repayment from some countries. Those measures are not unique: the Group of 20 has also pledged leniency to low-income countries burdened with debt.

What makes China's undertaking telling is that China has also been enlisted by the AU Commission to build the headquarters of the Africa Centre for Disease Control (Africa CDC) in Ethiopia. Notwithstanding some unsettled clarification with the site and time frame of the Africa CDC, the fact that China was chosen to lead the building of the centre says a lot about the intensity of Africa-China relations and Africa's confidence in China as a reliable partner.

China could also rest assured that allegations that emanated about surveillance of the AU headquarters did not considerably dent China's standing in the eyes of the AU.

The move to invite Ghebreyesus was not a perfunctory decision: it communicated a message to those who doubt the WHO, and it was also a vote of confidence in Ghebreyesus.

The US has been the most powerful and scathing critic of the WHO. Its criticism stems from what it perceives as the WHO's kid-glove approach to China's response to Covid-19. The decision by US President Donald Trump to withdraw financial support for the WHO is likely to have devastating consequences on regions like Africa that do not have enough endowments to deal with Covid-19.

The US administration has shown that it cannot be counted upon as a moral leader in the current international system. For that reason, Africa and China should adjust their expectations of US leadership. Trump will use the same method he used to clinch the 2016 election: employing nationalistic sentiment that borders on racialist politics and scepticism towards multilateralism. That might help him win the election in the short term, but the consequences of hamstringing institutions such as the WHO will be long-term.

Thus, the urgency of Africa's CDC cannot be overstated, and the AU should clear the bureaucratic haziness surrounding the construction of the Africa CDC headquarters. The two parties should also reassure the WHO, which should be the global leader in these trying times, of their support. The legendary Sino-African solidarity is needed now more than ever.

Covid-19 a huge hit to African economic growth: free trade can soften the blow

The Coronavirus pandemic has dealt a severe blow to Africa in multiple ways. Just a year ago, the world was gushing about Africa's economic growth, especially in small economies. That enthusiasm was not misplaced because Africa was one of the fastest-growing regions in the world. The 2.4% economic growth that Africa registered could easily have been higher if big economies such as Nigeria and South Africa had recorded more growth than they did.

The Coronavirus pandemic has punctured the enthusiasm of 2019. The African Development Bank (AfDB) has issued a supplement to its *African Economic Outlook*, published in January 2020. The AfDB now predicts that Africa's economic growth for 2020 might decline to -3.4% and that about 49 million Africans, mostly from West and Central Africa, could join the impoverished on the continent.

Those numbers are devastatingly scary. Already, the World Bank has noted that there is a chance that by 2030, Africa will face extreme poverty if the continent does not improve the calibre of its leadership and reduce economic risks. The African Continental Free Trade Area Agreement was established to marshal a continental approach to Africa's development. Our leaders have long known that Africa has a fair chance of success only if individual members have a vision beyond their borders. However, it took more than 55 years after the establishment of the Organisation of African Unity, which was later transformed into the African Union, for them to come up with an economic framework that could ease the passage of goods and services. That notwithstanding, the AfCFTA allows Africa to become more integrated.

Although intra-African trade is likely to mitigate the continent's susceptibility to the vagaries of global economic uncertainty, it is disappointing that intra-African trade still constitutes less than 20% of

Africa's total trade. That means that when Africa's major trade partners such as China and the United States are embroiled in trade fights, as has been the case, Africa suffers.

The US has been increasingly inward-looking, which might continue during the next four years if the Trump administration retains power in the November elections. The volatile nature of the current international system summons Africa to be more self-reliant. Still, for that to happen, the African Union has to be candid about certain things that hold the continent back. For example, the AU has to take a leading role in advising member states on how to deal effectively with Covid-19. It has to stamp its authority on countries that are using populist ways of dealing with the virus. Methods that are at variance with scientific counsel should not be tolerated.

South Africa is the 2020 chair of the AU, and its legacy for this year will be, to some extent, tied to how Africa copes with the Coronavirus pandemic. It does not help that its citizens have vilified the government's approach to Covid-19. Some argue that the decision to open schools while the virus is still on the rise is precipitate, irrational and illogical and comes close to Tanzania's refusal to secure its borders and restrict certain activities within the country as it tries to cope with the virus.

The small number of cases reported in Tanzania and Burundi is arguable because those countries are reluctant to carry out massive tests. Their logic is akin to Donald Trump's ludicrous allusion that a small number of tests translates into a small number of cases. The internal denialism of some countries will have long-term effects on the rest of the continent.

Apart from Tanzania and Burundi, who have gone against the grain of scientific opinion, Malawi is another country to watch. The recent rerun of the presidential election subjected many of its citizens to exposure to the virus.

All of that will have implications on how the nascent days of the AfCFTA will be facilitated. Countries with fewer cases of Covid-19 are likely to impose strict limitations on their borders. Those who have been vigilant in trying to curb the virus are also likely to limit travel from the errant countries. Such limitations on travel and the attendant restrictions on the transportation of goods and services will make the work of the AfCFTA a more daunting undertaking than it already is.

The African Union should shed the laager mentality, which is a relic of the bygone era of the OAU. The AU should be sterner in conducting continent-wide affairs, which, under current circumstances, entails firmly advising all member states to adhere to scientific wisdom as the guide for dealing with Covid-19. Evidence hitherto has shown that the US and other global players are either clumsily coping with the pandemic or are overwhelmed by it. That means that the AU should be the first port of call for the continent's challenges.

Tragically, more people will join the group of the extreme poor. That can be softened by a more assertive approach to Covid-19, which could facilitate a smooth take-off for the Free Trade Area, which in turn is likely to improve Africa's lot.

Taiwanese-Somaliland deal bad for Africa

Bizarrely, Taiwan has established diplomatic relations with Somaliland, a semi-desert territory on the coast of the Gulf of Aden. Ironically, Somaliland itself isn't recognised by any nation in Africa, while Taiwan was previously abandoned by almost all African countries, besides the Kingdom of Eswatini.

Somaliland emerged from Somalia's civil war that ended Jaalle Mohamed Siad Barre's dictatorship in 1991. Importantly, Taipei's provocative manoeuvre is bound to incense Somalia, the AU and China.

For the leadership in Hargeisa, that unwise move will alienate African countries, the support of whom Somaliland needs in its quest for statehood.

Equally, Taiwan's move is tantamount to creating animosity with Somalia and the AU countries from which it seeks support to participate in important international bodies such as the World Health Organization.

The Taipei-Hargeisa alliance comes amid the backdrop of escalating diplomatic tensions in cross-strait relations as well as between China and the US. That diplomatic manoeuvre by unrecognised actors on the continent poses enormous challenges.

First, it brings insecurity to the volatile Horn of Africa. For different reasons, many actors converge on the disputed territory of Somaliland. The Port of Berbera remains a strategic point of entry for the Middle East, comprising Saudi Arabia, Yemen, the UAE and Qatar.

Second, the former colonial powers in Europe, especially Britain, France and Italy, perceive Somaliland and the rest of the region as a significant source of migrants pouring into Europe.

Third, the US sees Somaliland through the prism of its war on terror. As Washington pivots to Asia with a focus on slowing the rise of China, it welcomes Taiwan's adventures in Somaliland.

The Taiwanese move in Africa worsens the island's relations with mainland China, and it takes place at a time when Beijing is dealing with endless disputes over borders and islands in the South China Sea.

Although Taiwan and Somaliland's sovereignties are not recognised by Washington, it surprisingly issued a congratulatory note on the newly established relations.

As expected, Beijing responded by stating: 'Such activities remain illegal and will never be recognised by the People's Republic of China. There is one China in the world. Taiwan is part of China, and the government of the PRC is the sole legal government representing the whole of China.'

The implications for Taiwanese involvement in Somaliland are dire for Africa. Somaliland will become a hot spot for the emerging New Cold War between the US and China. The Gulf of Aden will attract more foreign forces, complicating political dynamics in the Horn of Africa. As it stands, Ethiopia, the main anchor for peace and security in the region, remains unstable.

As Somalia stabilises, it will heighten its quest for the unification of territories it considers its own. Therefore, Taipei and Hargeisa ought to be careful in their premature diplomatic relations. They both have more to lose in playing global giants off in their quest for recognition.

4IR: opportunity to end male dominance

On 21 July, the prospects and potential of the Fourth Industrial Revolution (4IR) were central in a diverse and expert-driven virtual seminar organised by the University of Johannesburg (UJ) Centre for Africa-China Studies, co-hosted by the UJ Library.

Titled 'Gearing Africa for the 4IR', participation in the webinar drew from the UN, the Organisation for Economic Co-operation and Development (OECD), Huawei Technologies and the Youth Bridge Trust.

Attendees spanned several countries throughout the African continent, as well as China, France and Switzerland. The 4IR touches deeply on Africa because, in terms of demographic distribution – 60% of Africa's 1.25 billion people are below the age of 25 – the future belongs to Africa.

This seminar is in line with the one that took place last September in Cape Town titled 'Shaping Inclusive Growth and Shared Futures in the Fourth Industrial Revolution'.

The programme provided collaborative platforms for thinking about and tackling the challenges of our collective future. Technologies like Artificial Intelligence and the Internet of Things offer a new vision for economic growth, innovation, development and human well-being. The potential of 4IR in Africa is boundless. However, the continent suffers from an infrastructure deficit that significantly hampers technological progress.

To surmount that: the continent needs to note the trends of 4IR, learn from more advanced countries and identify partnerships that might be to its advantage.

There are certain conditions and trends that Africa could use to improve its lot, and those things do not require the entire range of 4IR. Small-scale agriculture is a case in point. It accounts for about 80% of the food production in Africa and 70% of jobs.

The use of data for precision in agricultural systems could be used to optimise farms, from anticipating natural disasters such as droughts and flooding to predicting the best time to harvest crops to anticipating outbreaks of pests and disease before they impact production.

In an era of ever-increasing challenges concerning ensuring food security, the application of data and smart farming practices is vital. Africa will need reliable and well-meaning partnerships to close the gap that exists between its technological advancement and that of other regions.

That will be a trying task because the current international system is fraught with disagreement on technologies, with countries such as the US and the UK ranged against more ambitious countries in the field of technology, such as China.

Apart from noting the trends and looking for good partnerships, Africa should also avoid challenges such as environmental degradation by adopting smart ways of doing business and industrialising. There is hope for Africa, as small-scale companies have shown resilience in the face of adversity.

4IR also allows us to end male dominance. Africa is the only continent where women are more likely to be entrepreneurs than men. Increasing access to e-commerce could have a positive effect on gender justice.

Zimbabweans, heal thyselves – don't expect any outside help

The unfolding narrative of the worsening crisis to the north of Limpopo involves new characters and intrigue. The current wave of instability started after citizens wanted to stage a protest against corruption and economic mismanagement. Their complaint was apposite because, for a long time, corruption in Zimbabwe has been endemic, and economic failure is evident at first glance.

President Emmerson Mnangagwa fired Obadiah Moyo, his then minister of health, for corrupt practices. That was an implied admission that corruption runs deep in the government. It is concerning that the government went on a violent rampage to foil the protest, harking back to the violent days of Zimbabwe under Robert Mugabe.

Whatever way one wants to view the current crisis, it resembles a floundering nationalist movement that has betrayed its liberation ideals. Once again, Zimbabwe faces its usual periodical flares, with this particular one coming at the worst of times, whether viewed internally or externally.

Despite the fanfare of a new dawn, ushered in by the military in upending Mugabe's almost four decades' rule, both Zanu-PF and the splintered Movement for Democratic Change (MDC) formations failed to find ways of uniting the country around a meaningful reconstruction. That goes to show that Mugabe's ouster was not an indictment on his leadership; it was a change of personnel, but business continues as usual.

The second-most crucial factor that distinguishes the current situation from previous disturbances is that the main guarantors of peace in Zimbabwe – mainly SADC led by South Africa, former colonial powers led by the UK and more importantly, the US – have lost the power to influence the situation. Zimbabwe has always been a mirror of South Africa's domestic challenges.

Former President Thabo Mbeki's handling of the Zimbabwe crisis during Mugabe's tenure was pejoratively called 'silent diplomacy'. Mbeki was constrained in being assertive towards Mugabe because Mbeki is a seasoned nationalist with reverence towards an illustrious nationalist of Mugabe's ilk. Second, the ANC and Zanu-PF also share certain ideals regarding land, the historical consequences of racism and global politics in general. Thus, condemning Zanu-PF would be like condemning a kindred spirit.

The perceived power of Pretoria to influence President Mnangagwa and Zanu-PF is eroding daily. While President Cyril Ramaphosa dispatches envoys Baleka Mbete and Sydney Mufamadi to Harare in an attempt to quieten the noise, his finance minister, Tito Mboweni, is preoccupied with the business of borrowing money from the IMF and the World Bank. That act of borrowing funds from the IMF was one of Zimbabwe's original sins.

Back in the late 1980s, Mugabe, through his then minister of finance, the late Bernard Chidzero, knocked at the doors of the IMF and World Bank. Although one is not privy to South Africa's envoys' message to Harare, it is clear that they are empty-handed. South Africa is in no position to talk about a financial rescue package for Zimbabwe.

What about the widespread view that South Africa commands power over Harare through the military, Eskom, SAA and other levers? Eskom can't keep the lights on at home due to sheer corruption and, similarly, SAA has no wings to talk about flying to Harare.

Even the esteemed envoys are more likely to have flown to Harare on other national air carriers. One only has to follow the Zondo Commission, which replicates Zimbabwe's Willowgate scandal of the late 1980s.

The land question over which both Zanu-PF and the ANC fought bitter battles remains mired in corruption in Zimbabwe and mainly indecisiveness on the part of the ANC. Zanu-PF has ultimately agreed to pay former white farmers for the land it once claimed would be taken without compensation – a current slogan in South Africa.

Britain and the US are too stuck in their unravelling decline to be counted upon to marshal any influence in Zimbabwe. The UK, outside the EU, carries no sticks or carrots of note to be noticed in Harare. With all of the above, one wonders what the envoys could say to Mnangagwa and the splintered MDC formations that would carry weight and warrant change. Not that the envoys bothered speaking to the opposition, which leaves the crisis in the hands of Zimbabweans to resolve.

If I could speak to Zimbabwean leadership, both in government and opposition, I would say, 'Don't expect external players to assist; they have no power and influence to do so. Please grow up and fix the crisis without delay, starting with the economy and good governance. Neither "flushing out" opponents nor "yellow revolution" will hold in Zimbabwe.'

In the end, the fate of Zimbabwe will be wrought by Zimbabweans. The outside world, starting with regional and continental bodies, has been ham-fisted in dealing with the situation. One of the regrettable facts about the so-called African agency and finding African solutions to African problems is that Africans are not candid about the indiscretion of fellow Africans.

It is only rarely that they call each other out, as happened in The Gambia when former President Yahya Jammeh reversed his decision to concede electoral defeat and wanted to stay in power. The Economic Community of West African States showed uncharacteristic firmness and forced Jammeh to vacate the presidency. Unfortunately, that has not been replicated in Zimbabwe.

The SADC countries are well aware of how the government in Zimbabwe has been handling its politics. However, SADC chooses to look the other way, thus condemning Zimbabweans to the state-sponsored terror that will drive millions out of their county.

Those realities should not discourage ordinary Zimbabweans. Instead, they should be emboldened in the realisation that they are the ultimate arbiters of their country's fate.

By Opinion / 15 September 2020

Africa must look East to revive economy post Covid-19

The African economy has been severely impacted by the ravaging pandemic and a reeling world economy. Covid-19 has driven economies into recessions and reversed many developmental plans, with more people left unemployed.

That begs the question, where can Africa look for lessons to kick-start its economy? China, more than any country, has made remarkable strides in containing the Coronavirus.

In a letter to the organisers of the 2020 China International Fair for Trade in Services (Ciftis), President Xi Jinping said: 'With the deepening of economic globalisation, trade in services has become a key part of international trade and an important area for economic and trade cooperation among nations, injecting new impetus into world economic growth.

'China cannot develop itself in isolation from the world, and the world needs China for global prosperity.'

China's economy defied the downward trend in most economies across the world. Despite Covid-19 and natural calamities that brought unprecedented floods in the southern provinces of Hunan, Jiangxi, Guangxi, Guizhou, Sichuan, Zhejiang and Yunnan, the Chinese economy grew by 3.2% in the second quarter.

That impressive economic growth took place at a time when the World Trade Organization warned that global trade is expected to fall by 13–32% this year. South Africa's economy shrank by 51% on an annualised basis in the second quarter. These are tough times that should compel the government, business and civil society to think differently in search of pragmatic adjustments in our relations with China and all other partners.

How can South Africa and the African continent take advantage of the trade opportunities in China in post-Covid-19? As it stands, Africa remains on the periphery of changes taking place in the global economy.

Given the well-established diplomatic relations between Africa and China through the Forum on China-Africa Cooperation, Africa must respond to President Xi Jinping's assertion that 'the world needs China for global prosperity'.

How can Africa tap into the Chinese service trade, which is growing at 7.8% per annum and contributing about US$775.6 billion (R12.9 trillion) to its GDP?

As the US-China trade war is expected to continue beyond the 2020 electoral cycle, Africa must be an alternative source for the much-needed goods from the booming service sector in China.

Relations between China and Australia, for instance, are in a downward spiral. Africa should, and must, expand trade in products such as wheat, beef, wine and other agricultural products. Plans should be underway in Africa on how to create a conducive environment for tourism in post-Covid-19.

Africa's tourism sector must coordinate in transforming how it attracts the large Chinese middle class. The endless power shortages in South Africa and many other African countries must be speedily addressed.

Similarly, questions about crime and unreliable modes of transport across the continent need urgent attention. Finally, African countries must improve the visa issuing process in line with a changing world in post-Covid-19. Perhaps subregions such as the SADC, East African Community (EAC) and Economic Community of West African States (Ecowas) must issue common visas to maximise the flow of tourists across regions.

By Opinion / 2 October 2020

Africa and China share common approach to climate change

Weather patterns across the globe are signalling that climate change will bring about catastrophic calamities to all of us. Increasingly, droughts, heatwaves, wildfires, rising sea levels, warming oceans, thawing permafrost, changing rain and snow patterns are adversely heart-rending.

Africa and China joined the rest of the world at the UN's 75th anniversary last month to highlight the urgent need for global responses to climate change. Prior to his address to the UN, President Cyril Ramaphosa warned that the world must 'swiftly reduce carbon emission and adapt to the effects of climate change; we will be facing one state of disaster after another for many years to come'.

President Xi Jinping of China avoided playing games demonstrated by his counterpart President Donald Trump on climate change. Instead, he pledged that China would achieve carbon neutrality by 2060, a move that has been commended and welcomed all over the world.

Although there are many notable differences in appearance, style and approach among Africans and China, they share a common position at the UN on climate change because it receives high priority within the Forum on China-Africa Cooperation.

At the Beijing Summit in 2018, UN Secretary-General Antonio Guterres highlighted the increased cooperation between Africa and China. He furthermore noted how Africa and China are pursuing what he considered as the 'two mutually compatible road maps': AU's Agenda 2063 and the UN 2030 Agenda for Sustainable Development in pursuance of the Belt and Road Initiative.

It is in that context then that Africa and China committed themselves to being environmentally friendly in the construction of mega-projects across the continent.

There are also many lessons Africa can learn from China's rapid rise. China is the only country in the world that has uplifted more than 700 million people out of poverty in four decades.

While Africa aspires to follow some aspects of China's development model, it ought to be mindful of the environmental impact of its development. China achieved its development at a very high cost to the environment, but President Xi Jinping's commitment to the Paris Agreement and setting clear targets of carbon neutrality by 2060 has made China a leading global champion on climate change, along with the African continent.

It must be recognised that Africa is the smallest producer of CO_2 emissions, yet, it is one of the most affected by climate change, and in recent years, it has had endless calamities caused by it. East Africa experienced swarms of voracious desert locusts amid Covid-19, threatening food security. The city of Cape Town was on the verge of reaching 'Day Zero' in 2018 due to a lack of rainfall. Mozambique, Zimbabwe and Malawi are still recovering from Cyclone Idai. Further afield, Ethiopia and Egypt face simmering tensions over the Grand Ethiopia Renaissance Dam on the Nile River.

Indeed, Africa should work with China and the rest of the world to prevent President Ramaphosa's prophecy from becoming a reality.

Pretoria News / 25 September 2019

SA, Nigeria must tackle xenophobia

The African Union declared this year the Year of Refugees, Returnees and Internally Displaced People. Africa has 6.3 million refugees and 14.5 million internally displaced people, which means that more than a third of the world's forcibly displaced people are in Africa.

Within Africa, South Africa is the most popular destination for immigrants, a trend that has often provoked incidents of attacks on foreign nationals.

This year's attacks on foreign nationals were distinct, coming in the year when the AU is focusing on displaced individuals and a year before South Africa assumes the Chair of the AU.

The attacks have also been distinctive in the way that some African countries have responded. South African enterprises were besieged and defaced in Nigeria and Zambia, and Madagascar and Zambia cancelled soccer matches they were supposed to play against South Africa. But the spotlight has mainly shone on the dynamic between Nigeria and South Africa, the continent's biggest economies, respectively.

Attacks on foreign nationals in South Africa are an expression of a frustrated citizenry whose hope for economic success after apartheid remains a mere aspiration. An ambitious and industrious migrant population is therefore perceived as a threat to prospects for economic progress. Thus, at the root of those attacks is the lack of economic transformation.

The influx of foreign nationals to South Africa is heavily influenced by conflict and economic despondency in countries of origin. Despite being a large economy, Nigeria remains a deeply crippled and crippling society. Its economic woes have been compounded by its ineffectual effort to foil violent extremism from religious fundamentalists, mainly based in the north of the country.

South African Reserve Bank Governor Lesetja Kganyago said at the World Economic Forum that South Africa and Nigeria's nominal economic growth

141

paints a bleak picture for Africa. At the same time, smaller economies show signs of progress and development. Petty competition and tit for tat reprisals based on xenophobic sentiment will further poison what is already a bleak dynamic for the two countries and Africa at large.

The implementation of the African Continental Free Trade Area Agreement promotes intra-African synergy wherein travel across African borders will be a primary factor. From that background, migration is inexorable and, if done correctly, could add towards developing the African continent. It is better, though, for conditions within African countries to attain a level that provides requisite comforts for their citizens. Such a scenario cannot be realistically imagined without impetus and leadership roles from Pretoria and Abuja.

Supporting each other could prove beneficial for those countries and Africa.

As long as the basics of economic percolation, good governance and social services are not secured, attacks on foreign nationals will continue, especially in South Africa – where citizens are not getting promising opportunities. In such circumstances, migrants further complicate an already fraught situation.

Mugabe's story a lesson for Africa

Despite his glaringly checkered record as a leader, Robert Gabriel Mugabe's life story remains one of pan-Africanism and hope for those struggling to repel neocolonialism. In death, as in his life, Mugabe casts a divisive incongruous persona.

The avalanche of obituaries written fails dismally to appreciate the fact that he was, by and large, a product of the same colonial system he fought hard to dismantle. Growing up in Kutama village, the young Robert Mugabe understood well that colonial education was critical to overcoming grinding poverty and colonial suppression. He became disciplined and studious, influenced by his mother and a Catholic priest.

Mugabe joined the famous Fort Hare University, a breeding ground for African political activism. The university boasts an impressive list of alumni such as Z. K. Matthews, Oliver Tambo, Nelson Mandela and Mangosuthu Buthelezi. Mugabe's first vocation seems to have been education and, as a response to that, he worked in Zambia and later Ghana as a teacher.

In Ghana, Mugabe met Kwame Nkrumah, a pan-African leader whom he admired and influenced his political orientation. The other influential figure Mugabe met in Ghana was his first wife, Sarah Hayfron. Those two people further influenced Zimbabwe's future leader's pan-African ideals.

Due to involvement in politics upon his return home in the early 1960s, Mugabe was imprisoned from 1963–1975 by Ian Smith's white minority regime. During that long period, Mugabe acquired additional academic qualifications that undoubtedly affected his ensuing years. Throughout the 1970s, he fought with nationalist movements in Zimbabwe and the region.

Although Mugabe's Zanu party was on the verge of defeating the white minority regime in Rhodesia, he joined Joshua Nkomo's Zapu at Lancaster House to find a peaceful resolution to the conflict.

Contrary to most misleading obituaries that portray him as a brutal dictator, he was revered in most Western capitals, especially in London. In the early years of his leadership, President Mugabe achieved great strides in education and health for his people. He stood firmly for regional integration in southern Africa and Africa, and he became a formidable voice within the Global South, advancing solidarity in the face of apartheid in South Africa and neocolonialism during the Cold War.

While recording those achievements, Mugabe brutally suppressed his opponents in Matabeleland Province (the Gukurahundi Massacre) while Britain and most Western countries stayed silent. Mugabe was knighted by the Queen and received numerous honorary degrees in the UK and US.

Throughout Mugabe's first decade-and-a-half, he protected appalling British interests, particularly land, agreed upon at Lancaster House. Mugabe's regime became a typical carbon copy of Frantz Fanon's depiction of the post-independence African state and elite.

When his progressive agenda to expand education and health was forcefully curbed by the International Monetary Fund and the World Bank through austerity measures, Mugabe lost the support of the urban elite. As Zimbabwe's war veterans became more restive because they had relied on state patronage, Mugabe embarked upon the land distribution programme to maintain political power and retain their loyalty.

What Africa can learn from Mugabe's journey is that leaders should be wary of not losing their ideals in their clamour to impress foreign interests. Mugabe was expendable to the West and experienced the ignominy of being tossed when he exhausted his usefulness. Another lesson is that power should not be maintained at all costs, especially if it is detrimental to the people.

Africa's future lies with Asia

The world sleepwalks into yet another recession triggered mainly by the raging US-China trade war and the senseless tensions over the future of globalisation, and Africa is a significant piece of the collateral damage from those global tensions. In June, the World Bank revised Africa's economic growth projection from 3.3% to 2.8%.

However, it seems that African governing elites are unacquainted with the impact that the trade war and its tensions (particularly in Asia) have on their economies, or they think that they are innocent bystanders.

The sad reality is that, given Africa's strategic relations with Asia, clearly shown by the vast trade volumes with the region, particularly China, it cannot afford to stand aside and watch.

There is an urgent need to realise that beneath the US-China tension lie elements of the struggles of the past: the attempt by Washington and, to some extent, Western countries to reassert their hegemonic position on the global stage. While the rise of Asia, and China, in particular, opened up opportunities for Africa to develop, that has unnerved the US and former colonial powers.

Africa's trade with the US and European countries remains critically essential; a rising Asia has, however, afforded the continent with an alternative source of investment. Therefore, events in Hong Kong, the nuclear crisis in North Korea, trade tensions between Japan and South Korea, and the South China Sea are of great importance to Africa.

Africa's history has always been intrinsically linked to that of Asia. At the height of colonialism and the Cold War in 1955, Africans and Asians gathered in Bandung, Indonesia to cement a strong bond against Western economic, political, cultural and technological dominance.

The ANC's Moses Kotane and Maulvi Cachalia represented the liberation movement at that gathering of African and Asian countries. After the Bandung Conference, the Non-Aligned Movement was formed in 1961, and today's Brics countries continue to strengthen the voice of the Global South on matters of global governance.

The current US-China trade war evokes images of the Cold War. However, under the prevailing circumstances, Africa is given priority rather than cursory attention, as was the case during the Cold War. Asian countries have been active in courting Africa, doing so through bilateral trade but also multinational initiatives, such as peacekeeping. China has done exceedingly well in stepping into the breach where other countries seemed to lose interest or hope. That has often happened through providing investment and taking up enterprises that have been abandoned.

The brand of ultra-nationalistic politics and the calibre of politicians gradually assuming positions of immense power in the Western regions gives Africa one more incentive to cooperate with countries that see potential in Africa.

The continent cannot afford to be left behind. By 2050, more than half of the global population of young people will reside in Africa. Therefore, Africa has a huge stake in how the future will be shaped and, ideally, it should be a leader in engineering a future that will secure the good of all humanity.

That could be done together with Asian countries that also have vast populations.

While the world's future would be better without the hatred that the US-China trade war has provoked, Africa has to work through the prevailing climate to be clear about what it wants and firm in the pursuit of its goals. The continent needs human development through education and economic growth.

Without taking sides, one objective observation is that China seems to have more prospects of helping Africa with that than the increasingly insular Western world.

Africa needs to make most of tourism surge

According to the World Tourism Organisation, Africa registered the highest tourist growth, on average, compared to other regions, with an increase of 8.6% ahead of the current global average of 7%.

In 2017 alone, Africa received almost 63 million visitors, which brought in an impressive revenue of US$37 billion (R568 bn). It is estimated that by 2030, Africa's tourist figure would have reached 134 million people. The market value of that sector stands at US$165 billion.

The AU's Agenda 2063 and the 2030 UN Agenda for Sustainable Development recognise the importance of the tourism sector's potential to absorb unemployment, preserve the environment and effectively manage resources.

There are numerous reasons why tourist numbers are rising on a year-to-year basis in Africa. During the last 15 years, the world witnessed a change in the global tourism sector trends, which included a significant shift from the usual Global North to Global South movement to a South-to-South movement of tourists.

The rise of the Chinese economy to number two in the world and particularly its 400 million-strong middle class accounts for a large number of those new tourists on the global stage. Africa has been a beneficiary of the Chinese tourists, as well as those from other emerging markets such as India, Brazil, the Gulf states and Russia.

In recent years, Africa and much of the devloping world have benefited from the tensions between China and the US. The flourishing partnership between Africa and China through Focac has facilitated and attracted more Chinese tourists to the continent.

Africa has some of the world's most impressive tourist destinations: renowned attractions in South Africa; the Okavango in Botswana; Victoria Falls in Zambia and Zimbabwe; the Egyptian Pyramids; the beaches in The Gambia and the migrations in the Maasai Mara in Kenya, to name but a few.

The continent also has many attractive unexplored and underdeveloped destinations in Ethiopia's ancient Christian kingdom, and there are other marvels in Sudan, Angola, the Democratic Republic of Congo, Rwanda, and the Kalahari and Sahara deserts.

While Africa makes remarkable strides in the tourism sector, there are many possible hindrances, too, and at the centre of those lies a lack of coordination.

There is a need to coordinate infrastructure, both physical and digital, to speak to one another for easy movement of tourists across the vast continent.

Tenuous security is also a blight. The abduction of Europeans by pirates off the coast of Somalia, perennial conflicts in North Africa and parts of West, East and Central Africa make it hard to develop a unified African brand as a tourist destination. Therefore, most African countries market their exclusive tourist destinations independently from the rest of the continent.

The images of chaos in Cape Town and Jo'burg work against the development of the tourism sector. The gang violence in Cape Town, which has brought the military onto the streets, sends negative signals to tourists, as do the police raids in Jo'burg and the reported crimes at airports, on Table Mountain and in Mpumalanga.

Although the outbreak of the deadly Ebola virus in the eastern Congo appears well contained, it is often reported overseas as if the whole of the African continent is affected.

To overcome those challenges, the AU and Regional Economic Communities (RECs) should work closely with the private sector to design strategies and tactics to attract more visitors to the continent.

We must boost intra-African trade, develop infrastructure

Infrastructure inadequacy remains a massive obstacle to Africa's economic growth, development and productivity. It is estimated that poor infrastructure cuts national economic growth by 2% annually and productivity by a staggering 40%.

Since its formation in 1963, the OAU, later transformed into the AU, has had the task of accelerating continental integration through infrastructure development.

The Lagos Plan of Action was the first continent-wide attempt by Africans to restructure colonial-era infrastructure to achieve pan-African unity and integration.

However, the LPA failed to take root, owing to several internal, regional and global political instabilities.

The Cold War and Bretton Woods Institutions' (IMF and the World Bank) policy of economic Structural Adjustment Programmes (SAPs) constrained Africa's ability to develop cross-boundary infrastructure.

In southern Africa, through cross-border raids in neighbouring countries, as well as supporting rebel movements such as Renamo in Mozambique and Unita in Angola, apartheid South Africa's policy of destabilisation frustrated attempts by the newly independent states to pursue infrastructure connectivity. From that background, Africa should shun meaningless debates and narratives emanating from outside its shores concerning the raging competition between and among its strategic partners.

The priority and focus for Africans should be on how to advance its interest to foster intra-African trade, productivity and integration and reduce poverty through infrastructure development.

The second significant move by the AU to deal with Africa's underdevelopment was when former President Thabo Mbeki, Olusegun Obasanjo of Nigeria, Abdoulaye Wade in Senegal and Abdelaziz Bouteflika of Algeria came up with the New Partnership for Africa's Development (Nepad).

That process led to the formation of the Programme for Infrastructure Development in Africa (Pida) in 2012. Pida was established to assist member states in coordinating cross-boundary infrastructure to increase intra-African trade and employment and achieve sustainable development.

That was to be done across four main infrastructure sectors: energy, transport, trans-boundary water, and Information and Communications Technology. Although there is notable development of pan-African infrastructure in many African countries, it remains unclear whether Pida will meet its 2040 targets. Efforts are underway to move from the initial Pida 1 to the second phase of Pida. What lessons were learned during the first phase? What should be done to improve infrastructure development in Africa?

The AU Development Agency, Nepad and the Economic Commission for Africa should first and foremost work closely with African centres of excellence, especially universities and the African private sector. While the AU and RECs design excellent infrastructure plans, they fail to be implemented at the national level.

There is a lack of capacity in many African countries to develop national plans aligned to the AU's flagship infrastructure programme defined by Pida.

In most African countries, infrastructure development is politicised, which leads to constant changes of infrastructure plans and priorities, and that is often accompanied by high levels of corruption, poor planning, inadequate skills and development finance.

Efforts should be made to strengthen the ability of African states to implement Pida's flagship projects to overcome those shortcomings. There is an urgent need to develop continental databases of the skills available and companies with the capacity to work with Africa's strategic partners in infrastructure development. The African diaspora should be fully mobilised to contribute meaningfully to that.

As Africa's developmental partners are many and varied, the AU must develop differentiated strategies and tactics to engage its strategic partners fully. For instance, the US and China do not pursue similar projects in Africa. During the second phase of Pida, Africans ought to pursue smart strategies to direct external partners in the development of its infrastructure.

There has been constant attention paid to the role of the US and China, as if they are the only players in Africa's infrastructure development. Still, many countries are investing in Africa's infrastructure, such as those in the Gulf, Japan, South Korea, Turkey, Russia, India and Brazil. Therefore, Pida 2 should be planned and designed differently. It must be people-centred with a particular focus on African youth and women.

In Pida 1, much emphasis was placed on soliciting advice from the World Bank and the consultancies in the developed world. There is no doubt that those players are crucial. However, Africa ought to rely on its people to develop its infrastructure. In my deliberations at Pida's seminar, I encouraged those in charge to avoid the exclusion of scholars, students and members of society in planning Africa's future.

Let's dare to dream

I spent the whole of last week researching Africa's industrialisation and the role of China in Kenya, and in the previous month, stayed in Ethiopia for a week.

Two cities during my visit, namely Nairobi and Addis Ababa, reconfirmed my confidence in Africa's developmental prospects.

During my sojourn in Addis Ababa, President Cyril Ramaphosa delivered the State of the Nation Address in which he outlined that, 'I dream of a South Africa where the first entirely new city built in the democratic era rises with skyscrapers, schools, universities, hospitals and factories.'

That envisioned smart city is in line with the Fourth Industrial Revolution theme that President Ramaphosa has been advocating since the advent of his administration.

Shockingly, the idea was widely dismissed as a dream not anchored in reality by the opposition parties and some academics. There is a famous Chinese saying: 'If your dream does not frighten you, it is not big enough.' Africa's developmental dreams are slowly being realised in Ethiopia and Kenya.

In the city of Nairobi, the Aviation Industry Corporation of China, a Chinese multinational, through a subsidiary, is erecting a Global Trade Centre: a smart city that will comprise more than 40 storeys of office space, 315 hotel rooms operated by JW Marriott, 51 service apartments for guests who might be staying longer than usual, a boutique mall, a large conference room and about four apartment blocks.

The completion date is 2020, and the smart city will be the first of its kind on the African continent. Its main target, multinational corporations, will undoubtedly be attracted to a convenient, safe and strategically placed node in the East African region.

If South Africa does not respond to the demands of the emerging era of technology, it will cede its place as the most industrialised economy and indeed will find itself lagging behind countries such as Kenya.

That bleak reality brings to the fore several challenges. One of those is convincing South Africans that if their country cannot manage existing cities, what is the rationale behind erecting a new one? Would it not be more plausible to first sort out the pressing challenges that bedevil existing cities before embarking on a new one?

Those who would answer such questions in the affirmative would find it hard to receive Ramaphosa's 'dream' smart city seriously.

Kenya's smart city is similar to the one that was once mooted for Modderfontein in the east of Jo'burg, which was to be established by Zendai Developments from China but was abandoned. Had it gone ahead, that smart city would have been bigger than its Kenyan counterpart.

Building that project was going to take 15 years from 2015 to 2030. However, due to a raft of challenges, such as disagreements between Zendai and the City of Jo'burg, the erratic nature of the rand and no clear assurance of real estate benefits, the project died.

The failure of the Modderfontein project provides a salutary lesson for those who espouse Ramaphosa's dream city. That the project failed should not prevent similar projects from being attempted.

The Ramaphosa government should be alive to the realities that confront South Africa. That could help with raising realistic expectations regarding the nature and scope of a smart city.

Though the task of establishing such a city will be inescapably demanding, the government should not shy away from daring to dream. A lot can come from dreams, but when awake, the content of dreams should be adapted to real circumstances of the waking mind, and that is what the ANC government should accept.

Reclaiming Africa's stolen heritage

The first Industrial Revolution coincided with the phenomenon of colonialism, which undoubtedly left visible scars on Africans and their civilisation. Art, in its various forms, was one demonstration of African advancement.

By its nature, colonialism denied the colonised anything that hinted at them possessing a mind that could rival that of the coloniser. That partly explains the looting of African artefacts which, up to now, are still confined in the museums of erstwhile colonisers.

Another facet of that looting was the religious element, the spread of which, in Africa, coincided with a spike in slavery and colonial activity. As they dismissed African art as heathenry, European missionaries had no qualms about destroying African artefacts they could not understand, while commandeering those they found attractive.

Many African countries have experienced being forced to adopt European names, as African names were thought not to accord with Christian nomenclature.

Wresting African art was not merely looting material things: it sought to deny Africa's place in the annals of art. Even more deeply, it almost obliterated an accumulation of African knowledge, thus engendering an invented lacuna in the continuity of African epistemology.

Artefacts are the vessels of the interconnectedness of all forms of African life. A few concrete examples could be adduced to emphasise the scale and manner of divesting Africa of its artefacts.

In extreme cases, Europeans made away with human body parts, which they kept as trophies. At the age of 45, Hintsa, the son of Khawuta, was decapitated on 12 May 1835 during the 9th Frontier War. The British soldiers took his head to Britain as a grotesque war trophy.

In 1868, the British seized Ethiopian artefacts, among them an eighteenth-century gold crown and a royal wedding dress, which were put into the custody of the Victoria and Albert Museum (V&A).

Condescending arguments have been made by Europeans, some of them opining that Africa is riddled with conflict and violence and hence cannot be relied upon to preserve the valuable assets. Others have argued that the artefacts could only be 'loaned' to Africa.

Amid such shameless arrogance, it is encouraging that Emmanuel Macron, the French president, whether driven by guilt gnawing at his conscience or by a genuine realisation of the injustice to Africa, has promised to make returning African artefacts to Africa a priority.

But lest this episode rank among countless others that were about Africa but driven by the outside world, the responsibility resides with Africans to not only reclaim the stolen artefacts but to realise just how valuable they are to African identity.

The agitation for decolonising school curricula should also include the return of artefacts, which are a crucial component of African epistemology. To give Africa's case the authority it deserves, it would help if the AU would be forceful in correcting a blatant injustice.

For as long as the said artefacts remain in European custody, there will be a gap in the continuum of African culture and knowledge. Repatriation will not be easy, and there will not be a shortage of chauvinists who have ordained for themselves the role of keeping artefacts for a seemingly incapable continent.

The continued holding of Africa's invaluable cultural materials casts a blight on European claims to seeking reparation for injustices done during colonialism. Yes, Africa has gained political independence, but as long as a crucial part of its history remains in the hands of former colonisers, the vestiges of colonial domination linger, and a part of Africa is still at the mercy of those who once conquered and ruled the continent.

Africa should not shun integration

Europeans' support for the main drivers of integration, such as open borders, a single currency, free movement of people, goods and refugees, is drastically diminished. Its support for democracy and human rights remains shaky.

It was thought that the more Europeans shunned integration, the more likely Africa's quest for it would come to a halt. Recent developments on the African continent show an opposite picture: Africa appears to be integrating at a much faster rate, at a time when Europe disintegrates.

According to the newspaper *This Day*: Nigeria, Africa's largest economy, will sign the African Continental Free Trade Area (AfCFTA) Agreement. That comes at a time when the AfCFTA has already been ratified by a sufficient number of African countries, allowing it to go into effect last month. When Nigeria approves it, as expected, Africa will negotiate from a position of strength with multiple trading partners around the world.

The current configuration of African states makes it difficult to negotiate individually with the US, China, Japan and the EU. African countries are too fragmented and cannot negotiate fair trading deals with strong partners, a classic example being Kenya, a country that is dealing with the US, in spite of having signed the newly launched AfCFTA Agreement .

Although the continent confronts numerous challenges, many countries are registering high economic growth and development. Ethiopia is a classic example. Its capital city, Addis Ababa, is demonstrating positive growth as more entrepreneurial activities take place. Improvements in Ethiopia's physical infrastructure have boosted regional trade in the Horn of Africa, as neighbouring countries like Eritrea, Kenya, Djibouti, Somalia, Somaliland and Sudan cement ties with that nation of 110 million people.

Meanwhile, 15 West African states have adopted Eco (derived from Ecowas, the Economic Community of West African States) as the name of the standard regional currency to be launched next year. That strategic move will go a long way towards easing former French colonies' dependence on France.

The adoption of Eco provides encouraging signs in the effort to move towards continental union.

The East Africa Community appears to be the most vibrant regional economic community in Africa. Kenya's President Uhuru Kenyata has announced that people from the region will only be required to carry their national identity cards when travelling to his country and will enjoy all the privileges afforded to Kenyans in seeking employment and accessing government services.

As the world enters an era of trade wars, high-tech cold wars and climate change, Africa needs to increase its integration efforts. A united continent has a stronger chance of fashioning better deals and relationships with partners. It cannot rely on the EU to stop the tide of African refugees to Europe. The dream of a United States of Africa, supported by all Africans, remains strong.

Many baby steps are being taken towards continental integration. To sustain the current achievements in Africa towards continental union, the AU ought to pay greater attention to building regional physical infrastructure, boosting intra-African trade and improving education and health for its people.

Unlike Europe, Africa cannot afford to shun continental integration, democracy and the process of globalisation.

The AU should continue to seek peace and security for itself. A united Africa could negotiate better with the big powers and represent its interests in global multilateral institutions such the G20 and the UN.

China-Africa trade expo a unique opportunity for Africa

Tomorrow and Friday, China will host the first China-Africa Economic and Trade Expo in Hunan Province. In addition to the more than 50 African countries that have confirmed their participation, several international bodies such as the UN Industrial Development Organisation, the World Food Programme and the World Trade Organisation will send representatives.

At least 1,000 Africans are expected to attend the Expo as guests or traders. The event is a further demonstration of the ever-growing Sino-African relationship, which traverses a gamut of issues, from historical similarities, political affinity and an economic reliance to the recently deepening people-to-people relations.

Last year, China-Africa trade reached US$204.2 billion (R2.9 trillion), up 20%, year-on-year. China has been Africa's largest trading partner for 10 years; thus, the Expo seems to be an expected initiative between two parties who have had an impressively growing relationship.

African entrepreneurs, alongside their Chinese counterparts, will showcase their products, no doubt culminating in bilateral trade and infrastructure agreements. The Expo will coincide with the G20 Summit in Osaka, Japan.

With the Sino-US trade tensions offering a cheerless backdrop to what portends to be an awkward Summit, issues concerning the developing world are not expected to dominate the debate. The Expo thus assumes even more importance in an international system that is currently undergoing a resurgence of ultra-nationalism, insular sentiment and antipathy towards immigrants who are not of Western provenance.

While that context is regrettable in an era where globalisation is expected to imbue the world with tolerance and acceptance of significant cities, primarily as cultural and national melting pots, it provides the developing world with an opportune impetus to concentrate on being principals and arbiters of their regions and affairs.

For almost the whole of Africa, China has become an indispensable player in helping the continent to surmount its myriad challenges. While Sino-African trade and economic ties have grown impressively, Africa remains rooted to the foot of the global food chain.

The opposite is the case with China, a country that, just four decades ago, was an agro-based, underdeveloped, poor economy but has risen to become the second-biggest economy in the world. By next year, China plans to eliminate poverty among its citizens.

Lin Songtian, China's ambassador to South Africa, often evokes the estimated 700 million people that the Chinese government has lifted out of poverty since the advent of economic reforms in 1978.

Prevailing circumstances have seen a surge in private Chinese and African citizens trading places between the regions to put down roots in their respective countries. While that is in kilter with the trend of globalisation, it has also precipitated tension that emerges from ignorance of each other, as well as racial confrontation and the scramble for economic opportunities.

Opportunities such as those offered at the Expo should be used to demonstrate China's good intentions as it relates to Africa. It's encouraging that since the onset of the US-China trade war, Africa's non-traditional exports such as meat, fruit, nuts and tobacco have improved. Intracen's Trademap estimates that meat exports to China from the Southern African Development Community have improved by 240%.

If that momentum is sustained, it will help Africa to invest more in land, climate change and hydro technology. The Expo will have a lasting legacy if it touches on that.

Trade accord in Africa in force, market unified

As the post-World War 2 institutions of global governance tear apart at the weight of anti-globalisation forces across the world, Africa has realised the long-held aspiration of continental integration.

The African Continental Free Trade Area Agreement is now in force after 30 May, and the unified market is to be officially launched on 7 July. But Nigeria, which is Africa's most populous nation and largest economy, remains outside of that continental market arrangement, which seeks to boost regional trade by reducing tariffs and freeing up businesses to operate unencumbered across the continent.

As a country that was an influential player in ending colonialism and apartheid and championing African unity, Nigeria's stance on the AfCFTA is curious. It could be indicative of a disturbing insular brand of politics that has led, among others, to Brexit.

Since the inception of the OAU, now the AU, in 1963, African leaders hoped for a time when the continent would enjoy more intra-African ties, thereby severing the divide-and-conquer stratagem that was used for the success and longevity of colonial conquest.

The 24 parliaments of the 52 countries who signed the agreement have finally ratified it, paving the way for the launch of the unified market. That is a remarkable achievement, as it takes place in an era in which regional integration schemes such as the EU are disintegrating.

The launch of AfCFTA will undeniably take place under an uncertain global climate defined by a trade war between the world's biggest economies: the US and China. It offers a single market for goods and services to 1.2 billion Africans with an aggregate GDP of over US$2 trillion (R29.2 trillion).

The United Nations Conference on Trade and Development, a trade organ of the UN, forecasts that the AfCFTA 'could bring US$3.6 billion in welfare gains to the [African] continent through a boost in production and cheaper goods'.

In the past three decades, Africans faced endless hurdles in their attempts to rival trade volumes with non-African partners. By deepening intra-African trade, the AfCFTA is an opportune initiative for bolstering the continent's prospects for trade success and renegotiating Africa's position in structures such as the African Growth and Opportunity Act. African Union members have to be candid about their strengths.

More industrialised countries could play a pivotal role in the beneficiation of raw materials. For an inexcusable length of time, the continent has remained an exporter of raw materials that, with increased industrial capacity and activity, could be refined and transformed into high-end products.

The AfCFTA is to the AU what the Lagos Plan of Action, crafted in 1980, was to the OAU.

The Lagos Plan of Action, despite its ideals, was hampered by human-made and natural conditions, ranging from trade barriers to droughts that undermined Africa's food production.

More than being a tool for economic ambitions, the AfCFTA comes with the promise of improving the movements of African citizens across the continent and boosting cultural exchanges. Thus, while the statistics in terms of trade forecasts after implementations are impressive, they will mostly ring hollow if the benefits do not trickle down to ordinary citizens and if Africans remain ignorant of and strangers to one another.

Even though a people-centred approach to implementing the AfCFTA would be the most ideal, Africa needs real champions to lead the cause of the continent. The first generation of African leaders, such as Kwame Nkrumah, Julius Nyerere and Nnamdi Azikiwe, were clear in their responsibility to end colonialism and secure African sovereignty. In their flawed way, they achieved some of their aspirations.

Hard lessons to be learnt from Algerian crisis

Why should the AU and Africans be concerned about events unfolding in Algiers? Algeria stands as an anchor state in Africa's quest to build strong bonds between North Africa and sub-Saharan Africa. It is also a crucial link between the continent and the Middle East.

Although Abdelaziz Bouteflika was not a democrat, he nonetheless represented the last few remaining nationalist leaders of the Algerian National Liberation Front (FNL) who defeated the French army in the Algerian Revolution. He contributed to Africa's renewal, such as transforming the Organisation of African Unity into the AU and the establishment of vital African institutions.

Mentioning Algeria evokes pride in Africans. During colonialism and apartheid, the Algerian Revolution embodied an ideal response to oppression. In their books, *Long Walk to Freedom* and *The Wretched of the Earth*, Nelson Mandela and Frantz Fanon, respectively, wrote fondly of Algeria as the symbol of liberation.

The Algerian Revolution fought between France and the FNL from 1954 to 1962 was seen by Mandela and Fanon as the heroic spirit of Africans to fight for freedom, equality and dignity in the face of white supremacism. The Algerian Revolution provided a template for fighting colonial oppression.

Why then is such a vast repository of African liberation careering towards an ignominious end? What will be the impact of the Algerian political and economic crisis for Africa and Europe? What lessons, if any, does the Algerian crisis teach nationalist movements?

The fear in the US, Europe and Africa is that Bouteflika's fall might trigger a civil war. There are signals of elite fracture that are in opposition to the rule of a dictator without any plan or unity of purpose among the opposition parties. The Algerian elite's failure to agree on a leader and development plan could open the country to hostile forces, namely terrorists and foreign powers, as was the case in Libya.

The impact of such a scenario will be felt across Africa: it will worsen the terrorists' activities in North and West Africa, and the crisis will add a significant number of migrants to Europe.

That situation provides us with several lessons for nationalist movements. Bouteflika's fall is a consequence of inept leadership, which, like the recent fall of Robert Mugabe in Zimbabwe, has shown the dismal failure by nationalist movements in Africa to mobilise their people towards national development.

While nationalists draw legitimacy from their heroic roles in the liberation from colonialism and apartheid, as governing movements, they should adapt to their changed responsibilities. Economically, for example, Algeria remains dependent on the oil and gas sector, and the dangers of such economic myopia have been exposed by the reduction of revenue for Sonatrach, the state-owned energy enterprise, from US$76 billion in 2008 to US$33.3 billion in 2017. It does not help that 30% of Algeria's GDP is from the oil and gas sector.

The leadership failed to expand freedoms to the populace. Fanon observed that the nationalist leaders tended to lose sight of ideals of freedom the moment they seized power. Thus, postcolonial leaderships fell short of being revolutions: they were replacements of the colonial personnel but left the oppressive edifice mostly intact.

That was the case in Zimbabwe. Postcolonial leaderships failed to imagine innovative ways to open new frontiers of economic development in education, health, rural development and the expansion of infrastructure beyond those left by the colonialists.

The regimes invested heavily in state security instead of their people, the result of which we have in Algeria – the catastrophic fall of the once gigantic symbol of African nationalism.

Cape Times: Opinion / 27 March 2019

Rural Africans still on fringes of priority

When natural disasters strike the poor, as Cyclone Idai did in Mozambique, Malawi and Zimbabwe, unsympathetic and biased narratives emerge.

The context on the ground and the global factors that give rise to such disasters get less attention. Inevitably, the effects of Idai could be placed in a historical context.

A significant number of Africans were consigned to rural areas and depended on subsistence agriculture to cater for their families. By necessity, that situation compelled rural Africans to settle next to areas that ensured a steady supply of water. In the event of natural disasters, areas around sources of water are the most vulnerable.

A knee-jerk reaction to that dynamic could be the evacuation of Africans from such areas and a massive urbanisation drive. That is an understandable temptation, considering that the 2017 UN Economic Report for Africa reports that 'urbanisation is one of the defining forces of the planet's twenty-first-century development. In 1950, the urban share of the world's population was 30%, but by 2050, it may well be 66%. Nearly 90% of the increase will be in Africa and Asia'.

Against a rash and wild clamour for urbanising Africans looms the fact that working the land is a crucial ingredient for Africa's development. The 2014 UN Department of Economic and Social Affairs lists economic and social development and environmental protection as the main pillars of sustainable development and multidimensional urbanisation as their crucial enabler.

However, lest Africans be tempted to embark on a grand-scale rural-urban drift, African governments should not only make it attractive for Africans to work the land but make it profitable too. However, that would require fortifying countryside existence against devastating natural disasters such as Idai.

Beyond the scope of national responsibilities, regional initiatives such as SADC's Climate Service Centre should be equipped with the requisite resources needed to predict the patterns of a globe that is perilously warming up. Even at the global level, initiatives such as the Paris Agreement are laudable attempts to mitigate the velocity of disasters that are an attendant consequence of global warming. It is thus disappointing that the US has walked away from the initiative.

The world has a jaundiced pattern of development and, hence, wealthier nations have, by nature, more formidable safety measures against the effects of natural disasters. It has also been established that such nations contribute more to carbon emission, which results in more impoverished countries suffering the effects of pollution wrought mainly by wealthier and more industrialised powers.

While the contribution in personnel and material from the UN and others is commendable, a more durable solution is to improve Africa's lot in terms of holistic development.

The picture typifying Africa has often been one of devastation. The dire state of Africa is a consequence of historical happenstance. However, successive African governments have also failed to shatter the socio-economic and political structure that was instituted by the colonial dictatorship.

That brings into perspective Frantz Fanon's prescient concern that postcolonial leaders will fail to engender a revolution that differs in substance rather than in colour and personnel from the colonial edifice. Rural Africans remain on the fringes of priority.

They are only paid fleeting attention during campaign trails or when emergency humanitarian intervention is needed, as is the case in the aftermath of Idai. There is no dignity in living such a life.

Natural resources will have to be harnessed in such a way that they will enhance development rather than be dreadful sources of danger to the people who depend on them.

It's important for Africa to speak with one voice

For different reasons, Africa features prominently in key strategic foreign policy documents of major powers and is fast becoming a centre of global strategic rivalry.

A close look at that renewed focus and interest in Africa by global powers shows the increasing importance of the continent in world politics, economy and security.

The emerging competition between those powers in Africa is centred on three major issues: the Belt and Road Initiative (BRI), future technologies and security.

While the AU does make periodic pronouncements on the prevailing global order, that often lacks the focus it deserves. For instance, there has been no serious study on the impact of the US-China trade war on the continent.

The world is changing. It is essential for Africa to speak with one voice on how it stays neutral regarding the emerging rivalry between big powers. More importantly, it must state its lack of interest in becoming the battleground of big powers in their competition for influence.

The rivalry among global powers in Africa goes beyond the case of the West and China.

Italian Deputy Prime Minister Luigi Di Maio has accused France of impoverishing Africa. He said clearly what most African leaders often avoid asking in public: 'If today people are leaving Africa, is it because some European countries, with France taking the lead, have never stopped colonising tens of African states?'

Despite the US's annoyance and irritation, Italy appears ready to join the China-led BRI.

President Emmanuel Macron of France, on the other hand, paid a four-day visit to Djibouti, Ethiopia and Kenya last week. His trip's main aim was to 'open a new partnership in economy' in Africa.

In Kenya, Macron said: 'Now, what we want to do, especially with our delegation of companies, is to be part of your new growth agenda. That is how France could be a long-term, credible economic partner.'

Africa has the fastest-growing population on earth, estimated to reach 2.2 billion by 2050. The continent is also urbanising quickly, with a notable rise in the middle class. It is abundantly clear, therefore, that the continent will be the second-largest consumer market after Asia for future technologies.

The tense competition, especially between the US and China, for such a vast market in Africa, should be a major concern for African leaders. The US has embarked on an aggressive drive to stop the roll-out of Huawei's 5G technologies in Australia, New Zealand, Canada, Japan and Europe. Numerous studies have pointed to the fact that Africans use cellphones more than landlines. It is just a matter of time before the big power battles over future technologies enter Africa.

Africa has had a terrible experience with extra-regional military interventions.

The Nato-led bombardment of Libya in 2011 and the assassination of President Muammar Gaddafi stand out as ghastly illustrations of how Africa's agency can be ignored by foreign forces in dealing with African affairs. From that background, the convergence of foreign military forces in Djibouti must be a massive concern.

Just so that we do not absolve Africa of all that has gone wrong on the continent, it is prudent to admit Africa's seemingly manifest ineptitude in strengthening the various dimensions of the continent, including human capital, political rectitude and economic progress.

Africa's weakness is its most formidable enemy and most significant hurdle in reinforcing African agency. African governments might protest against foreign intervention, but left on its own, Africa does not have the capacity, political will and moral example needed to solve the continent's complex and multifaceted affairs.

Africa could learn a lot from China

Africans account for a significantly high number of people wallowing in poverty worldwide, whether one uses the gross domestic product or purchasing power parity as essential standards of measurement. Therefore, eradicating extreme poverty should be the priority of African governments. Africans have to find ways of doing that to meet the number-one goal of the UN Sustainable Development Goals by 2030. However, Africa can learn some lessons from China.

The National People's Congress and the Chinese People's Political Consultative Conference gathered last week in Beijing for the Two Sessions meeting to review the government's performance in the past year.

China has single-handedly reduced absolute poverty by 66.6% since it opened up its economy in 1978. That has uplifted 700 million Chinese from poverty, making it the first country to meet the UN Sustainable Goals.

The Chinese leadership has set clear targets backed by policies and resources to eradicate absolute poverty by next year, which will make China a moderately prosperous nation by 2049.

In 2003, AU heads of state and government identified agriculture as a critical priority for development, leading to the adoption of the Maputo Declaration on Agriculture and Food Security. Henceforth, the Comprehensive Africa Agriculture Development Programme required African governments to invest at least 10% of their national budgets in agriculture.

The Malabo Declaration Principles set 2025 as the year in which Africa will eliminate absolute poverty, but Africa will not meet that self-imposed target.

Although there is notable progress in the performance of many African countries, poverty remains high. That means that African leaders ought to move beyond making declarations and targets that they cannot achieve. The lack of discipline, resources, political will, policy and regulatory frameworks are some of the reasons for the poverty alleviation targets not being met.

If left unabated, poverty will bring to a halt all of the other efforts to develop Africa. China has won the battle against poverty because the leadership mobilised the nation backed up by clear policies, resources, setting realistic targets and, more importantly, discipline. That is what appears to be lacking in Africa. Africa is rich in human capital, mineral resources and fertile land. It is time that Africans take a tough stance on the quality of their leaders.

Africa must pay special attention to anti-corruption efforts and redirect all of its resources to the battle against poverty. African citizens deserve an enabling environment that appreciates merit and does not frustrate their efforts. It would help successive governments to test the merit of some initiatives started under the auspices of previous governments. Consistency and stability have been crucial to China's rise. Africa could learn from that.

When Deng Xiaoping, the architect of China's miracle, famously popularised that aphorism 'crossing the river by feeling the stones', he meant that the future is pregnant with uncertainty, and China was well counselled to remain grounded. Another possible interpretation of that saying is that any initiative that a country weaves in its search to end poverty and surmount challenges has to emerge from the country's specific context.

Unfortunately, Africa has failed dismally in that regard because of policy susceptibility. The chronic dependence on mineral exports is one factor that has undermined the utilisation of Africa's most durable resources: its people and land. We can learn from China's recognition of adapting policies to local circumstances. Poverty can be ended by empowering Africans in all facets, diversifying economies towards land and ensuring that responsive leadership is in power.

Pretoria News: Opinion / 31 January 2019

With no saviour in sight, Zimbabwe needs help to save itself

Eighteen years ago, the so-called Mbeki-Mugabe Papers, purportedly penned by former president Thabo Mbeki, generated heated debates about the crisis in Zimbabwe. Some children born in that year, 2001, are now entering universities as first-year students.

How can one make sense of the history of colonialism and liberation to such a generation? Can that generation of students distinguish between the faces of colonists and liberators? Both colonists and liberators, in the eyes of those students, are underwriters of grinding poverty, corruption, misery, death and underdevelopment.

They have experienced neither colonialism nor liberation in their lives, but theirs is a life of struggle to survive at university. All they hear and see on the streets are protests for the end of the grinding poverty and state security brutality.

The 37-page Mbeki-Mugabe Papers, rejected outright by both Zanu-PF and the MDC, can be a useful starting point for the first-year student to understand the genesis of the Zimbabwean crisis.

It is high time that the Zimbabwean leadership across the political divide and civil society asked the question: How did the liberation narrative of the 1980s go wrong? Bob Marley sang in Harare on Independence Day in 1980 that Africans liberated Zimbabwe.

The political and economic crisis requires Zimbabweans to have a frank dialogue among themselves. Sadly, no amount of state brutality or opposition noise on the streets can resolve their crisis. As powerful and appealing as they are, the rhetoric of pan-Africanism, anti-imperialism, sanctions and boycotts will not bring stability and prosperity to Zimbabwe.

Pragmatism should inform Zimbabweans in their dialogue. That entails the refining and adjustment of the country's constitution to move into line with democratic norms and values. Institutions of good governance must be restructured and more people-orientated than their current state-centric nature.

The Mbeki-Mugabe Papers stated that the Zanu-PF government embarked on an unprecedented progressive programme to uplift the lives of the poor on borrowed money and donor resources. A decade into those programmes, the Soviet empire collapsed, which meant that Zimbabwe, like many other developing countries, had no other strategic partner to turn to in a bid to sustain its economy. The Bretton Woods Institutions – the IMF and the World Bank – applied the Economic Structural Adjustment Programme, which rolled back Zimbabwe's agenda. Confronted by the apartheid regime's destabilisation strategy in southern Africa and the failure to have an independent economic policy, Zanu-PF closed the democratic space and progressive language of liberation.

The former liberators became corrupt and turned against their progressive forces within trade unions, the urban elite and civil society. Resources meant for the people were deviated to satisfy the high living standards of liberators and the state machinery. In the past 18 years, the Zimbabwean story has moved from liberation to dictatorship and decay.

Although Zanu-PF, alongside the opposition, successfully dislodged the symbol of oppression and dictatorship, namely Mugabe, the political and economic crises continue unabated.

Zimbabwe faces a systemic problem that requires all hands on deck to resolve. Neither Zanu-PF nor the MDC can single-handedly resolve the current stalemate. As was the case in 2001, South Africa, Africa and the international community can only assist/alleviate the situation if Zimbabweans lead them.

Tackling Zimbabwe's problem requires holistic and pragmatic solutions led by Zimbabweans to seek a genuinely democratic path anchored in workable economic policies for liberation. The fantasy that one leader or one political party can resolve the crisis is just that.

In 2001, that was the message conveyed to the Zimbabwean leadership through the Mbeki-Mugabe Papers. It is also imperative to the 18-year-old first-year student that the Zimbabwean crisis started when the governing elite captured the state.

The Mercury: Opinion / 23 January 2019

Congo is trapped in a never-ending nightmare

Two fateful words uttered in the White House in August 1960, 'eliminate him', opened the floodgates to Congo's never-ending nightmare. Those came from the 34th US president, Dwight D. Eisenhower, regarding one of Africa's most outstanding leaders, Patrice Lumumba.

Barely five months later, Lumumba was murdered and his body dissolved in sulphuric acid, denying him a dignified burial.

That gruesome act brought the country under the control of the Western conspirators' preferred candidate, Mobutu Sese Seko. The people in the Democratic Republic of the Congo have not united through infrastructure development, peace and security since independence.

Then, after 18 years in power, President Joseph Kabila dragged his feet in leaving office, despite the 10-year term limit stipulated in the constitution.

The long-awaited elections were marred by irregularities. Sporadic violence in areas dominated by the opposition parties affected the conduct. That was worsened by an outbreak of the Ebola virus in Bikoro and Iboko Provinces.

When the ruling Common Front for Congo coalition candidate Emmanuel Ramazani Shadary was headed for defeat, opposition leader Félix Tshisekedi became Kabila's preferred candidate. Tshisekedi has since been declared the winner, despite reports from the Catholic Church of irregularities in vote counting.

Calls by the SADC and the AU to find a negotiated solution have been ignored by Kabila and Tshisekedi. Martin Fayulu has declared the process an electoral 'coup'. Although the elections appear to be an internal matter, they are critical to the SADC and the AU. First, the DRC remains the missing link in Africa's quest for development. South Africa and the continent have invested heavily in peace and security in the DRC and the Great Lakes Region.

Since the 1960s, the DRC has been the source of Africa's worst violence, including the Rwandan genocide. Silencing the guns would stabilise the entire region.

The SADC and the AU must ensure that the disputed elections do not reverse the significant gains made by the international community in maintaining peace and security.

The lack of a viable state would be a massive challenge for the government of Tshisekedi.

The DRC does not operate optimally for its citizens. It needs infrastructure connectivity, and it is vulnerable to external forces that benefit from chaos.

The DRC's rich natural resources are not benefiting its people or the continent. The country needs a stable government to harness those resources in line with regional and continental visions. But there's a lack of infrastructure. Inga Dam needs to operate at full capacity to boost the power grid. The country's water reserves can supply the region, alleviating drought pressure for countries like South Africa and Zimbabwe.

South Africa, the SADC and the AU should stay engaged to nudge the new leadership to embark on a reconciliatory and inclusive government. At the same time, existing peacekeeping efforts should be boosted.

What is happening in the DRC is not in line with SADC and AU electoral guidelines. Regional institutions of political governance need to devise measures that will compel member states to comply. Those should be punitive to bring about accountability and respect for human rights.

With supporters of human rights and democracy dwindling as the US battles with domestic woes and the EU seems to be weakening, Africans need to double their efforts to keep their peace. To that end, the SADC and AU should hold leaders accountable, and there is no better place to start doing that than the DRC.

AU must roll up their sleeves to set up Wakanda One

Is the AU leadership genuinely seeking to achieve Agenda 2063? Encouraged by the famous blockbuster movie, Marvel's *Black Panther*, the AU announced Wakanda One, a technologically advanced hub, as a symbol of the new African civilisation envisioned in Agenda 2063. It will be Africa's Silicon Valley or Shenzhen – the leading site for the Fourth Industrial Revolution.

Wakanda One seeks to turn Mosi-oa-Tunya (Victoria Falls), on the border of Zimbabwe (2,000 hectares), into Africa's technological epicentre, with Zambia (offering 132 hectares) to the project. The irony of the chosen country cannot be ignored: Zimbabwe, where citizens are on the streets violently protesting against the deepening economic and political environment.

Zimbabwe has not enjoyed freedom since 2000, mostly due to poor leadership. Both the ruling and opposition parties have abdicated their constitutional duties to outsiders, mainly former coloniser Britain and the Western world. It also contributes the most people in the world to the new African diaspora.

The Zanu-PF relies heavily on its liberation credentials and pan-African ideology to commit heinous economic and political crimes.

Similarly, the opposition MDC appears short on any independent thought or strategy. Both the ruling party and the opposition seem to be living in a wonderland, expecting outsiders (the SADC, AU and the West) to wave a magic wand to resolve their challenges instantly.

Those steeped in African history realise that there is nothing new about a Wakanda One project in southern Africa, particularly in Zimbabwe. The country's name, 'Dzimba-dza-mabwe', a Shona word meaning 'houses built of stones', was once such a great civilisation. The Monomutapa Kingdom spread from Great Zimbabwe in the Masvingo province, reaching Beira in Mozambique with satellites across southern Africa, including Mapungubwe in South Africa.

One wonders if the AU can entrust current Zimbabwean leaders with such a massive project. Wakanda One requires committed transformative leaders who can tap into the African indigenous knowledge system to marshal unity of purpose and the abundant resources on the continent and from the diaspora.

As in *Black Panther* (ironically written by a white man), the African diaspora mobilised resources to bring to life Africa's potential civilisation. It is therefore critical for the AU to stop watching movies and roll up their sleeves. First, Wakanda One cannot succeed in the colonial curriculum taught at our universities. It does not have enough African interest to give birth to such a new civilisation.

Second, Africans remain trapped in a colonial mindset, which devalues ubuntu in favour of Western notions of development, modernity and spirituality.

Third, Africans must declare corruption as a crime against humanity. If the high levels of corruption across the continent are not tackled head-on, they will hinder the Wakanda One project.

The idea of a Wakanda Village in southern Africa is long overdue. While drawing up plans for it, African leaders should stabilise the continent by prioritising peace and security. For Wakanda to be realised, those preconditions must be met.

The Wakanda Village idea can become a reality if Africa can pragmatically harness the rich historical experience of its former glorious civilisations, such as the Mali Empire (Timbuktu), Carthage in Tunisia, and Egypt, to name just a few. Africans need to cooperate with the international community to learn from other civilisations in Asia, the Americas and Europe. Africa can acquire knowledge and skills, particularly in science and technology. To actively participate in the Fourth Industrial Revolution, it requires projects such as Wakanda One.

Pretoria News: Opinion / 9 January 2019

Why Africa seems to favour China

Why do Africans seem to prefer or favour China? At a superficial level, it looks as if Africans only have relations with China, and other partners matter less. That perception emanates mainly from Western capitals. It is a perception, rather than a reality, driven by prejudice and fear of a rising China.

Regardless of the biased reports about Africa-China relations, Africa's relationship with China remains marginal compared with Africa's relationship with developed countries. The main reasons behind Beijing's perceived increased involvement in Africa are the dogmatic beliefs in the post-Cold War period that Africa's embrace of liberal democracy leads to development.

Despite the massive injection of resources to promote democracy in Africa by Western countries, there are disappointing returns on investments. The promotion of liberal democracy without tangible developmental support for Africa, such as favourable access to markets, trade, development of physical infrastructure, education and access to capital, have forced the continent to seek alternative partners. Thus, China's popularity in Africa comes from developed countries' neglect of the continent.

Western countries engage Africa for different reasons. Europe's focus is mainly motivated by the need to halt African migrants into the EU. And the US has a president with even less respect for Africa and its people. Its main objective is to limit China and Russia's diplomatic activities and economic investments.

In their quest for development, Africans entered into strategic partnerships with the major powers all over the world. African leaders realised that for the continent to maintain respectable economic growth and development, they required assistance and lessons from those who had achieved that.

What China has been consistently doing in its relationship with Africa since the formation of the Forum on China and Africa Cooperation is to show a serious commitment to implementing its pledges.

Africans realise that liberal democracy cannot prosper in the absence of development. What attracts Africans to China is the need for market access, physical infrastructure and learning from the successful programmes and policies of uplifting millions from poverty, as achieved by China.

Like the US in the 1960s, China is making impressive progress in science and technology, innovation, space and maritime issues.

Strategy and tactics guide Africans in their approach towards China. The lesson for developed countries is that liberal democracy cannot be parachuted into Africa without a developmental plan. When Africa embraces China, it does not inversely mean the rejection of Western countries and liberal democracy. Africa needs both China and the developed countries.

It is in this context that Africa will continue to seek close relations with all countries. Western countries should realise that there is no need to compete with China in Africa or to advance propaganda against China in Africa through the media. Africa does not always achieve its strategic partnership with China because AU goals are implemented at the member-state level. At times, member states' direct engagement with Beijing contradicts the AU's objectives.

Chinese involvement on the continent is starting to register positive results. A classic example is China's consultations with Ethiopia, Djibouti, Kenya, Rwanda and Egypt. There might be challenges in those countries' engagements with China, but tangible physical infrastructure and investments in manufacturing are improving lives in Africa.

Western countries can achieve similar results if they take Africa and Africans as serious partners and not mere subjects.

Where to from here for Zimbabwe?

The dust seems to be settling in Zimbabwe, with the transfer of power from one Zanu-PF veteran to another bloodlessly complete, for the most part.

Elite pacts or high-level negotiated settlements, as they are otherwise clinically called, are a recurrent theme in southern African history, especially in the settler colonies of South Africa, Kenya and Rhodesia/Zimbabwe.

Now that we once again see a resuscitation of Zimbabwe, the military clique and desperate opposition are eager to reap the Zimbabwean spoils of the carcass of the now former President Bob Mugabe. That, of course, comes at the expense of the masses of that country. It did not work in the past, and it cannot work now: it is 'out of sugar', so to speak, and will only serve to avert the real issue for Zimbabwe: the economy.

The critical failure in the international community has been in understanding that elite pact. Will it work this time? What will be different this time?

We need to shift focus with an understanding that the rush to elections, while symbolically appealing, will not get to the core of the deep-seated issues that need hard pragmatism.

The nature of the problem is indeed transcendent of Mugabe, the individual. Instead, it is a deep economic crisis that stems from both internal and external forces.

There have been bad policies by the liberation movement-turned-government: price controls, hyperinflation causing quantitative easing and currency mismanagement, which, at one point, saw the printing of Z$100 trillion notes as well as a lack of investor incentivising, to mention just a few – to the extent that, in 2008, the Zimbabwean inflation rate was estimated at a rate of 76.8 billion% per month.

And while more than one-third of the population is between the ages of 15 and 35, a staggering 86% of young people of working age are unemployed.

At the same time, however, the international community contributed to the crisis through, mainly, shock therapy measures by the World Bank and IMF. That concoction is what brought us here, which is not to say that Mugabe's repression played no role: indeed, it did.

But that repression was something that the Zanu-PF government inherited from British colonial rule and latter-day Ian Smith's Rhodesia and was never transformed. There were only cosmetic changes, which failed to address the economic problems of that country. Zanu-PF cadres were given custodianship of such a state and, as primed, carried out massive corruption and self-beneficiation.

In other words, they failed to carry out the people's demand for total liberation and emancipatory change in everyday life: the very promise that had made Zanu-PF so popular, to begin with.

Progressive steps taken in the early days were reversed by regressive ones enacted by an increasingly self-insulating political party. The saddest part of that, of course, is an opposition that is in tatters. They, like most of us, were caught off guard by the internal Zanu-PF coup that took place this month. Indeed, by every measure, they are not in control of the fast-paced changes in Harare. Their responses were predictable and, indeed, self-preserving. They have shown an immense eagerness for an elite pact with the generals in a 'government of national unity' arrangement.

Whether by design or sheer coincidence, their response – and indeed that of the people who took to the streets in their hundreds of thousands after the announcement of Mugabe's resignation – has played right into the hands of the military. They are now entirely caught up in the Zanu-PF cobweb, a fact that can only serve to strengthen the ruling party.

To begin with, it legitimises them and Emmerson Mnangagwa and a flawed transition of government. Second, that will buy them a much-needed grace period in which to rebrand Zanu-PF for a post-Mugabe period. And of course, although Mugabe will be out of government, Mugabe-ism will continue in his absence. The old guard is the same crop of people who protected him and his looting, from which they benefited immensely.

And, of course, there is the big question of whether the opposition has any chance of winning in a context where Mugabe is no longer president. They have based their message on negative campaigning; however, now that Mugabe is gone, the Zanu-PF may see a surge in popularity against the backdrop of an opposition party with no political and economic message outside of 'Mugabe must go'.

Now that he is indeed gone, the people may look in vain for a reason to vote for the Movement for Democratic Change (MDC) while the party searches in vain for a convincing reason why the people should vote for them.

Even if Mnangagwa, who is now preparing for an election next year, were to agree to a government of national unity, that would only play to his benefit, as it would allow him to parachute the opposition on his terms.

There is already a consensus in the country, the region and the world that it is better to deal with the devil you know. Working in his favour is the experience factor. Part of the reason that the Zanu-PF-orientated military staged the coup could be because they knew that Grace Mugabe would probably be widely rejected at the polls due to her lack of experience. Also, he is understood in the West and the East. He has already held a meeting with President Jacob Zuma before even being inaugurated, which can only be interpreted as a de facto blessing of his ascendency.

Pretoria, Washington and London are therefore respecting the transition but will continue to hope, until he proves them wrong, that he will move the country away from the path of repression (in which he was a direct participant) and become a converted democrat. Though rare, the likes of that were witnessed in Ghana under Lieutenant-Colonel Jerry Rawlings and Nigeria under incumbent president (and Major-General) Buhari.

The elephant in the room, of course, is whether Mnangagwa can go any distance in fixing the Zimbabwean economy, an economic situation that, in its decrepit nature, has become a caricature in itself. Does he have the right policies? Is he supported in the region and the world (critical external players with whom he will have to interact and cooperate in reversing the economic reality in Zimbabwe)?

As said earlier, the root causes of Zimbabwe's woes are both internal and external – the only convincing answer can therefore be that it is not only up to him and the policies he puts into place, pragmatism is needed to prevent a reversal to the failed policies of the past. An elite pact is not what Zimbabwe needs. There needs to be a people-centred approach to its problems.

The Mnangagwa government must find ways to first put a stop to the exodus of the people of Zimbabwe and the accompanying brain drain. It must equally think quickly and seriously about the experiences of other post-crisis nations in bringing back their diaspora (examples with lessons include Iran after 1979 and the ongoing campaigns of South Sudan and Lebanon to attract its people back), and that means understanding why they left in the first place. At the same time, it must tap into the skills and education those people might have returned with and act like a twenty-first-century government. Also, people do not need to return to contribute to their mother country meaningfully.

With remittances standing at twice the level of developmental assistance, taking advantage of the 'diaspora economy' may immensely benefit the country.

What of the international community? Let us be aware that these shifts in Zimbabwe are taking place at a time when there are significant withdrawals by countries across the world. For instance, as the Trump administration punts its America First policy, Whitehall is negotiating an exit from the EU. For South Africa, the primary issue is the official usage of the rand in Zimbabwe in a coordinated manner that is structured and avoids previous chaos.

The international investor community must be given incentives to return to Zimbabwe. Property rights should be guaranteed, as should fair trade, to avoid alienating investors.

A look at the agricultural sector, which is Zimbabwe's strongest, raises the land question and Britain. Britain, as a former coloniser of the country, must cleanse its original sins and respect the commitments that it made in the Lancaster House negotiations instead of passing the buck to South Africa.

And the EU and US must move beyond their neocolonial and somewhat racist policy of sanctions that seem to imply that they are more concerned with white farmers than with the Black people of Zimbabwe. The lifting of sanctions will give space to the new government to start afresh.

There should be incentives for them to achieve milestones in reversing the draconian policies of the previous government. To that end, the Heavily Indebted Poor Countries initiative, which was brought about for purposes of debt forgiveness for impoverished countries, should find application in Zimbabwe, failing which, what could be a renewed start might soon become consumed with paying off the atrocious debt of the Mugabe era.

Will any of those potential policies find application? There is a need to see Mnangagwa hit the ground running in the coming days.

To be watched most closely will be the countries that he will visit. South Africa is probably high on his list, as are China and the UK. Interesting will be the subjects of discussion in those meetings.

SA needs to act urgently to halt spiral in Burundi

The simmering political situation in Burundi is a reminder of the strategic shifts needed in South Africa's Africa Policy. Since the explosive events in Libya, Pretoria's Africa Policy (vision of ubuntu) has been ambiguous at worst and unfocused at best.

Burundi, a tiny country in the Great Lakes region, represents perhaps President Jacob Zuma's most successful case of mediation.

Since President Pierre Nkurunziza was returned to power for a third term by a limited pool of voters, 240 deaths from political violence have been reported. A former Nkurunziza ally, General Adolphe Nshimirimana, has been murdered, and there has been an attempt on the life of human rights activist Pierre Claver Mbonimpa. Both opposed Nkurunziza's bid for a third term.

The government's calls for people to give up their weapons have fallen on deaf ears. More than 200,000 Burundians have fled to neighbouring countries.

Although Burundi's constitutional judges said he was entitled to seek a third term, Nkurunziza ignored South Africa, the East African region and the AU's views that he shouldn't have done so, as it would violate the letter and spirit of the 2006 peace agreement that ended the civil war.

Those developments have constrained Pretoria's efforts as, technically, Nkurunziza won the constitutional court case heard by his appointees and held elections, although they were widely boycotted by opposition parties.

As an extra-regional player, South Africa relies on the East African Community (EAC) to intervene in Burundi. However, the EAC is home to illiberal presidents. Yoweri Museveni of Uganda, Paul Kagame of Rwanda and Joseph Kabila of the Democratic Republic of Congo (DRC) are trying every trick in the book, including violence, to alter their constitutions to extend their stays in power beyond two terms.

Under Nelson Mandela and Thabo Mbeki, South Africa relied on major powers to cajole Burundians into moving towards a resolution. Zuma's move to consolidate South-South cooperation has unintentionally alienated traditional partners like the US and EU. The reaction of those countries to Burundi's undemocratic trajectory appears to be no longer in sync with South Africa's Africa Policy.

The US and EU have imposed sanctions on four Burundians suspected of being behind the violence. They have also suspended their aid in opposition to Nkurunziza's bid for a third term.

Although South Africa has good relations with Bujumbura, it will be difficult for Pretoria to persuade Nkurunziza to follow the 2006 peace agreement without the full support of the East African Community, the AU and the other big powers.

The longer the Burundi crisis remains unresolved, the higher the chances that it will unravel South Africa's Africa policy.

In the Great Lakes region, conflict in one country tends to spill over into other countries. Zuma needs to deploy an experienced envoy to the Great Lakes region urgently.

The East African Community and the AU need to adopt a specific position. Tanzania's newly elected John Magufuli, who has started his presidency on a high note by opposing corruption, could be a neutral player in mediation.

South Africa ought to send a clear message to Nkurunziza, Kagame, Museveni and Kabila that suppressing political opponents through the barrel of a gun does not bode well for Africa.

That message should have the support of the international community. The US and EU, however, are inconsistent, as they condemn Nkurunziza but praise Kagame, Kabila and Museveni as architects of peace.

Regardless of the dangerous direction taken by Nkurunziza, Pretoria can influence all players in Burundi and bring them to the negotiating table.

South African Politics

Mboweni fixated on two countries

In recent days, Lesotho and Rwanda, both tiny African countries located in southern and East Africa, respectively, have generated heated debates in South Africa.

At the centre of those debates is none other than South African Minister of Finance, Tito Mboweni, an influential member of Cabinet with strong views on a wide range of issues beyond his portfolio.

Apart from managing the national finances as assigned by President Cyril Ramaphosa, Mboweni has endlessly generated intriguing news headlines in areas such as tinned fish recipes, the type of shoes he wears, performance in the bedroom. In short, he has demonstrated the boldness to 'tread where angels fear'.

For different reasons, Lesotho and Rwanda are perhaps the minister's favourite topics. A question might arise as to whether his expressed views on those countries undermine his fellow Cabinet ministers in charge of matters concerning external affairs. The other question that requires answers is whether the minister is failing to separate personal experiences and feelings from matters of the state.

When it comes to the minister's opinions on issues concerning Lesotho and Rwanda, one is afraid to categorically state that he fails dismally to reconcile his personal experiences and feelings from national and continental agendas. On Lesotho, his recently expressed view is shy of openly calling for the unification of Lesotho into South Africa or the southern Africa region.

That idea is nothing new: it has been advanced by Basotho people and scholars. It is also a solution that the author favours for resolving Lesotho's perennial economic and political crises. However, it is politically inappropriate for a Cabinet minister to openly express his personal views outside government policy.

Basotho people ought to deliberate independently about whether they go for unification with South Africa or the southern Africa region. The minister appears to be ahead of the Basotho people, his government, SADC (Southern African Development Community) and the AU (African Union).

Those utterances on Lesotho have the potential to undermine South Africa's future mediation efforts and economic interests in that country: e.g., South Africa relies heavily on Lesotho's water. The unification option favoured by the minister might appear attractive but it has its limitation: Lesotho is not the only failing state in the region.

What about Zimbabwe or Malawi? South Africa must work closely with neighbours to come up with better foreign policy options than simply swallowing poorly governed neighbouring countries.

Which brings us to Rwanda, another favourite country of our minister. Rwanda is different from Lesotho. It is a country that is increasingly showing remarkable resilience and recovery after one of the twentieth century's deadliest genocides.

Mboweni, like many observers of Rwanda's 'economic miracle', is fascinated by the sheer foresight of the Rwandan people to develop from a low base in a region marred by state collapse, as is the case in the DRC (the Democratic Republic of the Congo). There are indeed endless good stories from Rwanda that one cannot dismiss. Equally, it is essential to state that Rwanda is run by a benevolent dictator who, although he is a bosom friend of our Minister of Finance, openly undermines South Africa's sovereignty by deploying his murderous operatives to kill his political opponents on our shores.

President Paul Kagame has also undermined South Africa's interest in the DRC. Mboweni's tweets ought to comprehensively grasp those dynamics in both Lesotho and Rwanda. Perhaps he should consult his counterparts in Lesotho and Rwanda to fully understand their positions before he presses 140-character tweets expressing complex opinions on foreign policy.

IEC a laudable example to Africa's democracies

Fast-forward to 2019, and the transition of governments is no longer a signal of an impending genocide and civil war but a contested race for bureaucratic power and office, as it should be.

From only eight nations in 1990 with inclusive franchise rights for their populations, to 18 in 1996 who were considered democratic, in 2019, 55 member states of the AU are obligated to hold regular and democratic elections.

In 2019 alone, 26 countries have planned elections, which is unprecedented for Africa. However, challenges linger. According to the BBC, 15 democracies in Africa are 'defective', meaning that there are democratic elements and institutions of government and governance, but they cannot be trusted and are therefore illegitimate. That means that although a country may hold an election, politicians tamper with electoral commissions and cannot deliver free and fair elections. The courts that should decide on the fairness of an election are also captured and offer biased decisions.

Various countries have developed electoral commissions from South Africa's example. Since its inception in 1996, the Independent Electoral Commission of South Africa (IEC) has offered a blueprint to developing and developed democracies on how to conduct free, fair and credible elections.

Today, we see a maturing Africa in terms of democratic culture and representative politics – even in countries that have endured autocracy and dysfunctional democracies that maintained dictatorships.

In 2017, Uhuru Kenyatta won a second term in Kenya ahead of his opponent Raila Odinga. But the Supreme Court found that the election conducted by the Independent Electoral and Boundaries Commission (IEBC) was fraught with irregularities and illegalities.

In November 2017, after the new Commissioner of the IEBC and the Supreme Court affirmed a second election free, fair and credible, Kenyatta was inaugurated.

In Zimbabwe, Emmerson Mnangagwa's Zanu-PF had its election victory challenged in the courts by MDC leader Nelson Chamisa, who cited counting irregularities at the polling stations. In August 2018, the Supreme Court of Zimbabwe dismissed Chamisa's claims, and Mnangagwa was inaugurated.

But the biggest success story was in the Democratic Republic of Congo where, for the first time in 40 years, a successful democratic election was held. Joseph Kabila relinquished power to Felix Tshisekedi amid claims that the Constitutional Court had heard objections from the opposition about election interference. Crucially, the international community, including the AU and SADC, called for the opposition to comply with the DRC's constitution and laws.

In South Africa, a marginal dent in the 2019 election was smaller parties claiming that the IEC had insufficient control in the voting process and that some people had voted twice, some stations had not opened on time and scanners were malfunctioning. Those claims were not substantial enough for independent observers and the IEC to repudiate the entire poll.

The ANC was the outright winner, and the main opposition parties conceded. The professionalism and seeming impartiality of the IEC offers a laudable example to other electoral agencies in Africa who, for good reason, haven't enjoyed voters' confidence. Only when such agencies are credible will Africans believe in elections.

IOL News: Opinion / 2 May 2019

China initiative offers major trade opportunities for SA

The Second Belt and Road Initiative Summit concluded in Beijing last week and will go down as a defining moment of the twenty-first century.

China built a formidable coalition of willing nations to endorse the Belt and Road plan that will significantly reshape global trade and relations. It will also be remembered as the first international summit to have exposed major cracks within developed Western countries since 1945.

For instance, Italy, Greece and Switzerland broke ranks with tradition and joined the Belt and Road Initiative (BRI). In their calculations, the BRI presents more critical economic opportunities for their people and countries than rhetorical noise from Washington, Bonn and Paris.

The UN, the World Bank and the International Monetary Fund have acknowledged that, if effectively implemented, the BRI stands as a significant global economic stimulus that could revive the faltering global growth that is projected at 3% in 2019 and 2020.

President Xi Jinping's opening speech to 40 global leaders from Asia, Europe, Africa and Latin America struck a conciliatory tone. He candidly addressed the concerns of those opposed to the BRI. Myriad problems are emanating from Western capitals – ranging from the perception that Beijing violates the well-established global rules set by Western powers, to the BRI, which is seen as China asserting its hegemonic ambitions.

However, the march of the BRI seems inexorable. Through the Forum on China-Africa Cooperation and deep bilateral relations, Africa has somewhat retained a special place in China's foreign policy. However, China would be negligent not to invest more energy in courting countries that are more developed, industrialised and offer more economic promise.

Thus, while Africa could still hold on to its role as a supplier of mineral and energy resources to China, it might not benefit efficiently from the BRI initiative. The onus to participate in the BRI in a way that boosts Africa's hard and soft infrastructure is primarily the responsibility of the continent.

Africa featured prominently in the summit with AU chairperson President Abdel Fattah el-Sisi of Egypt relaying the continent's voice on the BRI to the delegation.

However, South Africa, Nigeria, Angola and many other countries on the continent were conspicuous in their absence. As a Brics member and key contributor to Africa's peace and security, South Africa ought to be an active participant in the BRI.

More than most African countries, South Africa's economic growth remains sluggish. Last year, it registered an attenuated growth rate of just 0.8%.

In his budget speech in February, Minister of Finance Tito Mboweni estimated South Africa's real gross domestic product growth would be about 1.5% this year, 1.7% for 2019 and 2.1% for 2021. While those forecasts manifest improvement, they still fall short of South Africa's potential of a 3.7% growth rate as estimated by Mark Appleton of Ashburton Investments.

Coupled with good governance, which automatically wins people's trust in leaders and public institutions, and taking advantage of initiatives such as the BRI could be of immense help to South Africa.

South Africa's notable inactivity in the BRI is due to the country heading for an election that does not guarantee a vast majority for the government. After the disastrous Jacob Zuma presidency, it is expected that the ruling party will try to convince the electorate that Zuma's departure indicates a shift towards honest leadership.

It would be advisable, however, that after elections, South Africa rethinks its stance on the BRI with the possibility of being an active participant.

Due to the size of their respective economies, Nigeria and South Africa have assumed a natural leadership role in Africa. Initiatives such as the BRI and the African Continental Free Trade Area could only benefit Africa if the two economies feature prominently.

SA's golden opportunity to uplift Africa

At last, South-South cooperation is no longer empty rhetoric. The New Development Bank (NDB), known as the Brics Bank, has held its fourth annual meeting in Cape Town. It has demonstrated its assertiveness in closing the infrastructure financing gap in developing countries.

Subhash Chandra Garg, India's finance secretary, said, 'The NDB was set up without capital from developed countries; the time has come where the NDB should not just be for Brics but for the world.'

Contrary to the controversial views propagated when the NDB was established – that it would replace the World Bank and International Monetary Fund – it has no intentions to do so and doesn't have the capacity to achieve that.

But it is worrisome that the full operation of the NDB shows the rise of South-South cooperation institutions operating parallel to the existing developed country-dominated institutions.

That further opens a vast gulf between developed and developing countries on critical issues of infrastructure financing. It also makes it extremely difficult to come to any global consensus on how to grow the global economy.

As it stands, the NDB operates on a new set of norms and values on projects and loans. The World Bank and IMF adopt an intrusive and interventionist approach prescribing to countries policies to follow, but the NDB tends to steer clear of the internal domestic affairs of countries. It prefers to look strictly at the developmental impact of the loans and adherence to sound financial governance.

This NDB meeting came against the backdrop of worrying global events such as Cyclone Idai in Mozambique, Brexit, US politics, and the waning of international institutions such as the UN and World Bank.

Brics countries – Brazil, Russia, India, China and South Africa – have successfully established a parallel development finance institution. There was no need for the NDB, aside from the fact that the developed countries refused the entry of developing countries into the Bretton Woods Institutions.

To fully understand Brics and its NDB, one has to go back to the Bandung Conference of 1955, where Asian and African countries met. The Conference was attended by ANC representatives Moses Kotane and Maulvi Cachalia, and the issues raised – fairness in trade, development finance, access and management of the World Bank and IMF for developing countries – remain.

South Africa's participation in Brics, the NDB and potentially the Asia Infrastructure Investment Bank (AIIB) has a great chance to ease Africa's ability to access more favourable infrastructure finance. South Africa must promote the inclusion of African countries in Brics and the NDB. Lessons from Cyclone Idai underscore the fact that the lack of infrastructure in southern Africa impacts adversely in times of disaster.

As South Africa benefits from its NDB membership, it is crucial to ensure that Africa overcomes the infrastructure bottlenecks affecting continental integration. In that context, South Africa should join yet another vital development bank, the AIIB.

The agreement for South Africa's membership of the AIIB requires Parliament's ratification. The AIIB is already bigger than the World Bank and is poised to play a critical role in infrastructure financing in Asia and Africa. As the world changes, as seen by the rise of the Global South institutions such the NDB, South Africa and Africa must ensure that the continent is not left behind in the global advancements, particularly in infrastructure.

The NDB and AIIB will be game-changers in developing Asia and Africa. The focus is on hard infrastructure, but it is crucial to consider the funding of soft infrastructure such as schools and hospitals in Africa, prioritising the absorption of the youth in its operations.

Cape Times: Opinion / 6 March 2019

Ramaphosa must make the 'neighbourhood' a priority

The Southern African Development Community appears relatively stable and peaceful. However, beneath the veneer of stability lie challenges that could unravel decades of freedom from colonial rule and apartheid.

It comes as no surprise that President Cyril Ramaphosa has devoted more time and energy to the SADC than any other part of the world. He has visited the capitals of Angola, Namibia, Botswana and Eswatini (Swaziland) on state visits.

The SADC remains a priority of South Africa's foreign policy. How a country manages the affairs of its immediate neighbourhood goes a long way towards demonstrating its ability to excel at the global level.

South Africa owes Angola a colossal debt for its sacrifice of human capital, finance and infrastructure in the liberation of South Africa and Namibia. Ramaphosa visited Luanda to underscore that South Africa would work with Angola to uplift the lives of the people in South Africa and Angola through trade and increased interaction of people in business. As with South Africa, Angola had a peaceful transition of power.

Like Ramaphosa, President João Lourenço is dismantling corruption, which defined the rule of his predecessor, José Eduardo dos Santos. South Africans are no longer required to secure visas to enter Angola on a short visit. That has a powerful potential to boost tourism and trade between the two countries.

Similarly, Namibia and Botswana peacefully elected new heads of state, free of the violence in many African countries. Ramaphosa registered the importance of those countries in the drive to increase intraregional trade, peace and stability. His visits are primarily informed by South Africa's desire to create a conducive environment to bring peace and security in line with SADC and AU agendas for industrialisation and Agenda 2063.

The recent visit by the president to Eswatini, however, poses challenges. It remains an undemocratic state under the monarchy. The president might have noted worrying tendencies in Eswatini, primarily the suppression of the will of the people to choose their leaders.

Pretoria must raise the issue of human rights to ensure that Eswatini's governance of elections is in line with SADC and AU guidelines. Western powers are ignoring political events there, in favour of Zimbabwe and Venezuela, due to the resources in those countries.

In a week, the president will embark on perhaps his most challenging state visit – to Harare. The situation there requires an urgent and comprehensive response involving role-players in Zimbabwe, Africa and the world.

Zimbabwe has been a divisive country because of how then-President Robert Mugabe's actions and rhetoric alienated traditional trade partners and brought the role of punitive and conditional relations among nations under the spotlight.

Western actors imposed sanctions to force the government to pander to standards of Western demands, politics and economics. South Africa has had to play a delicate role as it seeks to justify why, during apartheid, the ANC used sanctions to isolate the Nationalist government. It seemed not to advocate the same for Zimbabwe.

While the West has been punitive, China, driven by its non-interference principle, has been a timely partner to help Zimbabwe.

The ANC has argued against imposing sanctions for two reasons: the first is the potential damage they might have on an impoverished country, and the second is that it cannot assume the role of a hawkish player against a fellow African government.

Thus, while South Africa can demonstrate what good leadership should be, it is unfair to expect it to be punitive or imperious in trying to salvage the Zimbabwean situation.

Fuel price can be better managed; we have options

Another fuel price adjustment is on the cards, but this time it is in the form of a massive decrease. One cannot help wondering at the timing of that, given that the lucrative silly season is just a few weeks away.

Usually, when consumers are expected to tighten their belts, spending slows down. But that slowing of expenditure spells disaster if it coincides with the period most synonymous with reckless spending, which can and does help kick-start the ailing economy.

From March, fuel has increased from R14.20 to the current R16.85. The Christmas break comes with massive cash injections into the economies of KwaZulu-Natal, Limpopo, the Eastern Cape and the Western Cape, with modern-day migrant workers heading home for the holidays.

However, that will likely not happen if food and fuel prices increase. Politicians see fuel as a sort of trump card that they hold against the people, but when their decisions directly affect our pockets, we dig deeper into questioning them.

South Africa has options. For decades, we have had the opportunity to source our oil from countries here in Africa, especially Angola and Nigeria. Since 1994, the continent has been championing building regional economic communities as building blocks for continental integration and intra-African trade as envisioned by Ghanaian politician Kwame Nkrumah.

Currently, only 20 per cent of all African trade constitutes trade among Africans. Regardless of many gatherings in Addis Ababa of our heads of state and government to deliberate ways and means of uniting Africans, AU member states trade more with countries outside the continent than with their fellow African countries. It appears that we still cannot find ways to fix that.

Perhaps there is a need to educate ourselves about the reasons for choosing foreign oil from far-away partners. Still, beyond that, there are even more urgent questions around the costs of energy and development.

No country can promote and drive development without the reasonable pricing of oil. Beyond the transport conundrum (public transport increases, private car expenses, diesel pricing) we also fall prey to the rising prices of goods and follow-on increases. That directly affects the efforts of the government to build small- and medium-sized businesses. Unemployment remains alarmingly high at 27.5%, and South Africa has one of the highest unemployment rates for youth in the world.

Let us not forget, three years before the current VBS bank heist, there was another oil robbery staged in South Africa by those leaders we entrusted with our votes. The South African Strategic Fuel Fund (SFF) illegally emptied 10 million barrels of its oil reserves at US$28 per barrel while the global price of oil was at US$40 per barrel.

South Africa should seriously consider abandoning importing oil from the unstable and increasingly volatile regions in the world, such as the Middle East. The US could go to war with Iran. Saudi Arabia's regional destabilisation policy in Yemen and across the region will accelerate with no end in sight. That means that South Africa should find alternatives to mitigate against high oil prices.

To do so, oil robbers who staged a heist three years ago at the SFF should face the might of the law. Efforts should be taken by the government to manage our oil reserves efficiently. Pretoria should work closely with the Angolan government to build oil pipelines and boost trade between the two countries. The Inga Dam in the DRC should be completed. While doing that, perhaps add another water pipeline to Johannesburg before its Day Zero kicks in.

Personal
Political

Pretoria News: Opinion / 11 March 2020

Top role in struggle of two women

As the world marks International Women's Day, it is timeous to highlight the role played by two forgotten revolutionaries, South African Nokutela Dube and Russian Nadya Krupskaya.

Those two lionesses are among many brave women in the world who played critical roles in liberating their countries. However, their efforts were silenced by their patriarchal comrades.

Nokutela (née Mdima) Dube was born in 1873 in Inanda, South Africa, four years after Nadya Krupskaya's birth in 1869 in Saint Petersburg, Russia. Unfortunately, today those women are remembered as wives of their partners: Nokutela as the wife of the founding leader of the ANC, John Langalibalele Dube, while Nadya is referred to as Vladimir Lenin's wife.

Other than marrying those famous and powerful men, Nokutela and Nadya shared many similar traits and experiences. They were both brilliant scholars and leaders who contributed significantly to the struggles against colonialism, gender inequality, racial discrimination, patriarchy and, in Nokutela's case, apartheid. Yet, their life stories remain unknown.

While Nokutela was working with her partner John Dube in establishing *Ilanga lase Natal* newspaper and opening the Ohlange Institute in South Africa, Nadya worked with workers on defending their rights in Russia.

We celebrated International Women's Day on 8 March. Nokutela and Nadya provide us with a classic example of how the role of women in society is undermined and eroded not only by the oppressors outside but also by their comrades.

Although Nokutela was honoured with the Order of the Baobab in Gold, that was a century after her death when she was buried in an unmarked grave. Women's roles in the struggle against colonialism and apartheid on the African continent continue to be relegated to footnotes.

It would befit President Cyril Ramaphosa to flag the heroic roles played by Empress Taitu Betul, Mbuya Nehanda, Josina Muthemba Machel, Queen

Njinga and many more women when he chairs the AU in South Africa. There should be a concerted effort to reform that organisation and all other continental institutions of governance with a focus on ensuring women's representation and gender-sensitive policies. The starting point should be the national liberation movements that played a significant part in suppressing roles played by their female comrades.

Violence committed against women didn't end in 1994; it has continued under the post-apartheid government, and there are numerous statistical records to prove that. African women occupy fewer senior positions in government, business and our universities than men, and African women, particularly those residing in the former Bantu states, remain trapped in an oppressive patriarchal governance system of traditional leadership. In short, women still endure age-old oppression.

Goal 5 of the UN's Sustainable Development Goals calls for gender equality and the empowerment of all women and girls. Incidentally, the United Nations Under-Secretary-General and Executive Director of UN Women is Phumzile Mlambo-Ngcuka, a South African politician who served as Thabo Mbeki's deputy president from 2005 to 2008. Mlambo-Ngcuka and Cyril Ramaphosa have a difficult task when it comes to women empowerment, as they come from the developing world where the fortunes of women have always been in a precarious state. Furthermore, they come from South Africa, a country where all forms of abuse against women – economic, professional, physical and sexual – are scandalously rife.

The task at hand should be multipronged. There should be swift punishment for those who propagate or support that scourge of abuse. Women who have risen against trying odds to contribute massively to their countries and the world should be celebrated with the same gusto as their male counterparts, and a battle must be waged against the malevolent effects of patriarchy.

We've done well but we can do better

Watching President Cyril Ramaphosa delivering Monday night's weekly update to the nation on Covid-19, I wondered about the mental health of our leaders and our people.

Thomas Schaefer, the finance minister of Germany's powerful state of Hesse, committed suicide. Volker Bouffier, the state premier of Hesse state, said that Schaefer was worried about 'whether it would be possible to succeed in fulfilling the population's huge expectations, particularly of financial help. He apparently couldn't find a way out'.

What does that mean for our leaders and people facing even stiffer challenges than Germany, Italy, Spain and the US?

Ramaphosa conveyed the message to the nation that it would be better to take drastic preventive measures than to wait for Covid-19 to ravage our people. There is no need to put our leaders and ourselves on suicide watch. However, it is crucial to seek an alternative strategy that suits our environment. It is frightening to ask questions about the availability of beds, ventilators and protective gear.

The economy faces more challenges. Finance Minister Tito Mboweni has alluded to the fact that the country might knock at the International Monetary Fund's door for a financial bailout. Therefore, it is in the interest of all stakeholders in the war against Covid-19 that shielding our people from the pandemic remains the best option.

What are some of the mistakes made in the fight? What is to be done to alleviate the situation? While Ramaphosa and his Cabinet are doing an excellent job in keeping the nation informed, more can be done. The government's message is competing with an avalanche of fake news. Bring Deputy President David Mabuza on board to provide mid-week updates. That could be coupled with the involvement of other critical role players at provincial and local levels. The top-down communication is working but could be enhanced by messages from other relevant stakeholders within civil society and the private sector.

At times, people tend to mistrust politicians in favour of religious and traditional leaders. The SABC has sufficient capacity to better translate messages into the 11 official languages in a simplified fashion.

The pledge of funds (R3 billion) from our business community for small enterprises is an excellent move. Should the lockdown go beyond 21 days, there will be the need to assist many people with food parcels. That will be a difficult task, given the challenge of corruption. The military can help by ensuring that they are accepted into policed communities: a soldier carrying a food parcel in their hand instead of only the gun on their back would be more welcome and appreciated by the residents.

The military and police should also be seen to be a peaceful, helpful force who provide information to communities while enforcing law and order. Where there has been an abuse of power, those responsible must be held accountable for their actions.

Telecom giants such as Vodacom, Cell C and MTN can distribute relevant, vetted information. In countries such as China, technology played a critical role in curbing the spread of Covid-19.

More importantly, it is vital to consider the expertise of psychologists to ensure that the mental health of communities is prioritised. That is important for our society emerging from the traumatic colonial and apartheid eras in which the language of violence occupied a central role.

In the days and months to come, more lessons should be learnt from the pandemic. Building a robust public health infrastructure must be made a top priority. The days of mimicking Western nations and undermining public health infrastructure in favour of profit-driven health care are gone.

Covid-19 might not be the only pandemic the world will face. We should never be caught off-guard again.

Why pray for your flock when you can prey on them?

Africans have always had contradictory relations with religions – even from 400 years ago when sailors landed in the Cape with the Bible in one hand and a gun in the other. Missionary objectives have always been double-pronged, maybe even single-pronged, with one being a smokescreen for the other.

African resources have been plundered and ploughed in the name of religion in either natural resources or people. Some religions have played a significant role in the liberation of the people of Africa.

There is a rise of predatory practices in most religions that must be stopped immediately to allow the continent and its people to prosper.

Fast-forward to the present day, and we're seeing a resurgence of that devastating playbook being orchestrated by US, Nigerian, and even South African dogma, promising people profit and prosperity for blind loyalty.

That new wave of evangelism is particularly attractive to Africans because it resonates with the clairvoyant nature of African spirituality and the materialism of modern-day reality. People are raised from wheelchairs as 'evil' spirits are vigorously expelled from them.

People's wages and livelihoods are offered as tithe sacrifices for membership and to buy favour and solicit fortune from God in a sort of twisted investment scheme.

There seems to be a covert partnership between those groups and some African governments because, during all the madness and abuse, action against the churches is generally slow, when there is any. It's a sort of campaign against independent thought – understandably because the concept is a threat to church and state, especially in Africa where democracy is such a foreign concept.

The churches maintain a flock-like discourse focused on miracles and metaphysics among the population, which conveniently keeps governments free of accountability to the people.

Such was the case of a Pentecostal church in western Uganda in a community ravaged by the HIV/Aids pandemic, where a pastor attributed people's sickness to immoral and irresponsible sexual conduct and pronounced that the disease would be cured by prayer. That leaves no room for governmental intervention programmes for treatment and prevention, only prayer. Closer to home, a child perished at Pastor Paseka Mboro Motsoeneng's church in Katlehong last year because her mother took her to the church instead of a hospital for treatment.

After the pastor failed to heal the child, paramedics were called, but the child died on the scene. Even in a simple medical emergency, people have been conditioned to trust the Church and its antics to heal, with devastating consequences.

We've seen gangsters and thugs declare themselves deities so they can fly under the radar of reason. They have tricked communities into channelling the little they own to those con artists for salvation – or even just to be with like-minded people led by a spiritual guide.

Some pastors have raped women and girls and kept them indoctrinated and at their beck and call. They've made people eat grass and snakes and drink petrol and sprayed insecticide on their faces – all in the name of deception.

People's desperation acts like blinders: they cannot perceive anything but the wild fantasies of those pastors. When there is a constant and pervasive threat against a people, when does the government decide that regulation is required and enforced?

When do governance structures decide to protect vulnerable people who are being tricked by liars and deceitful men out of their pensions, livelihoods and daughters? Is it by design that the guardians and protectors watch idly by while women are forced into harems as unwilling concubines for social acceptance?

The most vulnerable are the little girls and women from low-income homes with no fathers. Possibly because they're desperate for a better life and a strong male figure – and if that man happens to be aligned with God, it sounds like a dream. But soon it becomes a nightmare, where the girls don't object out of fear and stay bound by that and paranoia.

A church is meant to be a place of solace and peace from the painful and evil perils of everyday life. But the agents of death who are seemingly mushrooming all over the most vulnerable of African communities are eroding that notion and being assisted by governments who are supposed to fortify their people's well-being.

What are they to do now? To whom must they turn?

Pretoria News, Opinion / 17 October 2018

Is Pik Botha deserving of a state funeral?

We all witnessed how heroes can change into villains when freedom fighters the globe over got drunk from absolute power and changed their tune to enslave the very people they were meant to liberate.

But can the opposite be true? History has not only given us an abundance of fallen champions from Stalin to Fidel Castro to Robert Mugabe but also folks like Oskar Schindler, who saved over 1,000 Jews during the Holocaust. People like that are hard to come by, those who swim against their tyrannical grain. Was Pik Botha one of them?

That pertinent argument raged on social media from last Friday morning when former Minister of Foreign Affairs, Roelof Frederik Botha, known as Pik, died in his Pretoria home.

The consensus was that he, like the rest of the apartheid machine's apparatus, should be thrown into a hole and forgotten as soon as possible.

But then the better-heeled (and -read) among us were quick to reference his dual role as a foreign minister for the Nats and the ANC under Mandela. Indeed, his work under Mandela cannot and would not wipe his bloody slate clean from all the operations that were run in and around southern Africa during the so-called Bush/Border War against the MK and Swapo operatives. But they cannot be ignored, either.

Pik's politics drew him as a man conflicted. His domestic policies were aligned with the strict conservative and racist apartheid ideal; while abroad, his hardline policies gave way to diplomacy and peacekeeping.

In 1988, he was instrumental in brokering and signing the peace treaty between Angola, Cuba and South Africa in Brazzaville, Congo; in Namibia, he was the central figure who organised a meeting in Zambia between Swapo's Sam Nujoma and South West Africa's Pretoria-appointed administrator Willie van Niekerk to discuss the end of the Border War. The conclusion of those discussions resulted in the independence of Namibia. Finally, his first flirting with diplomacy and indeed peacekeeping was his attempt at brokering peace between the ANC and the apartheid state by having Pretoria sign a non-aggression pact between South African and the People's Republic of Mozambique called the 1984 Nkomati Accord.

That noble act and others like it solidified Botha as an ally in the liberation of the African people. In the year 2000, Botha declared his intention to join the ANC, after his native National Party was all but dead. His reason was that he believed that he could do more for the representation of the Afrikaans minority within the party than from outside.

So, if lesser beings like *Die Groot Krokodil* were offered Category 1 state funerals – with a sobering intervention by his widow to make it a quiet affair – and the de facto dictator of Bophuthatswana, with his track record of aligning with Afrikaner hardliners and senselessly murdering innocent people in a bid not to relinquish power in the '90s in opposition to democratic transition, being offered a provincial funeral in early 2018, then indeed individuals with clear humanitarian track records deserve more than a 'bon voyage' and good riddance from South African society.

Monuments, memorials, statues and state funerals are the rites reserved for the truly special among us. They are symbols of appreciation chartered for those who make a positive difference in our collective lives and who we would be poorer without. So, using those lenses, Robert Mugabe would be lauded as deserving of honour and so would Mangosuthu Buthelezi. Why, then, would Pik Botha not be accorded the same?

Gluttony and crass materialism killed ubuntu

The relentless pursuit of wealth has manifested in a system of devastating capitalism. In a sense, the new world order has become about people who will do anything for profit, power and prestige – no matter the source.

South Africa's collective financial institutions, from banks and insurance companies to audit firms – and the organisations that regulate them – have been the shining beacon of good governance, debunking Africa's poor reputation in that regard. Few in Africa have been able to improve commercial infrastructure in the transition to independence from colonial rule.

South Africa built up fiscal structures that were even better than the ones Western countries had left behind. But in December 2015, that reputation and the systems that upheld it were rocked to the core.

The president had already been stained as morally flexible due to his court appearances for everything from fraud to rape, and international trust waned. It was for the state institutions, the airtight Constitution and the private sector to keep the politicians honest. So when the finance minister with a proven track record and recognised tenure within the Treasury was replaced by a virtual unknown, the markets reverberated.

If our development is based on the global community doing business with us – which relies on international confidence in our financial systems – then the weakening of those systems spells the decline of our development. That leads (as in Nigeria and the DRC) to economic and political instability.

Gluttony and crass materialism have poisoned men. One possible cause of that breakdown in values once synonymous with the identity of people of African descent is the concept of wealth-ism.

Wealth-ism is the idea that wealth is the primary determinant of superiority. That view is usually held by the poor and generally distorts perceptions of ethics and morals. Previous beliefs around life, family, community and country are replaced by the pursuit of money; ubuntu is a source of shame.

The crescendo of that degeneration was the suspension of the notorious Gupta accounts at all four major banks and the implication of KPMG and McKinsey in some of the family's business operations that were supposedly defrauding the South African public.

The pillars of financial independence were implicated in a crime. On 13 June last year, Moody's rating agency downgraded South African banks to a 'negative outlook'. On 24 November, Standard & Poor's followed suit and downgraded South Africa to junk status. The final nail was the World Economic Forum's Global Competitiveness Rankings fall from grace for South Africa, fuelled by the decline of quality in auditing and reporting standards. We held the top, for years, but in 2017, our rank dropped 14 places to 61 out of 138 countries.

The Independent Regulatory Board for Auditors said that the decline is informed by economic indicators for rating agencies: the strength of the securities exchange, efficacy of corporate boards, protection of minority shareholders' interests, decrease in the strength of investor protection, and firms' ethical behaviour. That collectively represents an economy's vital signs and, in 2017, those indicators, coupled with governmental economic policy uncertainty, drove South Africa backwards.

This year hasn't seen much of an improvement, with further slippage as the country discovers details around ministerial involvement in Gupta-linked business irregularities from the Zondo Commission. Now, the daunting task of returning international confidence and, more importantly, national moral decency to South Africans is imperative to drive growth, both personal and commercial.